KIPLING'S ENGLISH HISTORY

RUDYARD KIPLING

KIPLING'S ENGLISH HISTORY

poems chosen and presented
by Marghanita Laski

Hìc pudor, hìc morum probitas hìc aulica suada, Et lepor, & vitæ generosa modestia gliscit.

BRITISH BROADCASTING CORPORATION

Kipling's English History was broadcast in five parts on BBC Radio 4 in May 1973 and repeated in August 1973 and June 1974. The producer was Helen Fry. The readers were:

John Arlott: *Cold Iron, The Craftsman, Edgehill Fight, The Looking-Glass, Mine Sweepers, Norman and Saxon, 'Poor Honest Men', Puck's Song, A Tree Song.*

Bob Copper: *Chant-Pagan, The Dawn Wind, Eddi's Service, The Land, The Anvil.*

Rosalie Crutchley: *En-dor, The Looking-Glass, My Boy Jack, A Smuggler's Song, A St Helena Lullaby.*

Hannah Gordon: *Harp Song of the Dane Women.*

Tony Hall: *A Death-Bed, The Dykes.*

Godfrey Kenton: *My Boy Jack.*

Monty Modlyn: *The Absent-Minded Beggar, The Dutch in the Medway, Mandalay, The Sergeant's Weddin', The Widow at Windsor.*

J. J. Murphy: *A Pict Song.*

Rosamund Nelson: *Soldier, Soldier.*

Joseph O'Conor: *Danny Deever, 'Follow Me 'Ome', The Irish Guards.*

Joanna Jane Powell: *Gertrude's Prayer.*

John Samson: *A Death-Bed, The Explanation, Gentlemen-Rankers, Gethsemane, Heriot's Ford, The Holy War, The Land, 'Rimini', The Roman Centurion's Song, Soldier, Soldier.*

Gary Watson: *The American Rebellion: After, The Children, The Coiner, Dane-geld, The English Flag, Epitaphs of the War, 'For All We Have and Are', James I, Jane's Marriage, Mesopotamia, The Mother's Son, Philadelphia, The Queen's Men, The Question, Rahere, A Song to Mithras, Sir Richard's Song, The Storm Cone.*

Published by the British Broadcasting Corporation
35 Marylebone High Street, London w1m 4aa
© Marghanita Laski 1974 and Mrs George Bambridge
isbn 0 563 12650 7
The poems in this selection are taken from
The Definitive Edition of Rudyard Kipling's Verse
and are reprinted by permission of Mrs George Bambridge,
Macmillan of London and Basingstoke and Eyre Methuen Ltd
Printed in England by John Blackburn Ltd, Leeds, Yorkshire

CONTENTS

with places and dates of first publication

4 TOMMY ATKINS AND THE YEARS BEFORE ARMAGEDDON

5 THE GREAT WAR AND AFTER

INTRODUCTION

It was missionary zeal that led me to suggest some programmes of English history, illustrated and illuminated by the poems of Rudyard Kipling. I felt confident that these programmes could give pleasure to many people and, not least, to myself, and I can now say, with confidence, that I was right.

I thought there would be pleasure in what is now, perhaps, rather an old-fashioned approach to English history: that is, straightforward story-telling made vivid by poems and verses and jingles that were lit by pride in our heritage and, sometimes, by concern for its fragility. Then I was hoping to communicate pleasure in Rudyard Kipling's poetry to people who believed they didn't like it; and pleasure in poetry-in-general to people who believed they didn't care for any poetry, no matter what.

These would be enough reasons for suggesting the programmes, but there was another one, at least as important to me. I don't, on the whole, like the way poetry is presented on radio, and, in particular, I don't like the standard poetry-reading voice, which I think separates many listeners from poetry. Almost all poems read on radio are read in Gentry English, that is, the standard voices of well-educated upper-middle-class people in South-East England. This is not the English that most people in Britain speak. It is not even the English that most British poets have spoken; and though it is the English that Kipling himself spoke, it certainly isn't the one he imagined for most of the poems we used in these programmes.

So what the Producer and I tried to do was to have each poem spoken in the English dialect that was, so far as we could tell, ringing in Kipling's ears when he wrote it. Sometimes this dialect is, most appropriately, Gentry. More often, it isn't.

In printing these poems with my commentary on them, I haven't altered the scripts so as to suggest that they were intended to be read privately rather than listened to. On the contrary, I should like readers of this book to imagine the poems being spoken. With each poem I have given the dialect in which it was read, but it might be fun for readers to try some of them in other dialects.

But though reading to oneself can be satisfactory for people who already rely on poetry, for reading aloud, a voice that can manage the right dialect isn't nearly enough. To give pleasure to listeners great skill is needed, and all but one of our readers – the young boy who asked the questions in 'A St Helena Lullaby' – were very skilled indeed. Many of them could manage more than one dialect and, somewhat to our surprise, it was necessary to ask this of them. For it appears that the overwhelming preponderance of the Gentry dialect in skilled poetry-reading has led to a dearth of skilled poetry readers in other dialects, even in some of the dialects most widely spoken in Britain.

My own test for judging the best reading was that this was the one that gave me a shiver in the top of the spine and perhaps a tear in the eye as well; and I discovered that many of us who were working on the programmes and many listeners used the same test too. I hope it will sometimes work when the poems are read quietly to oneself.

In broadcasting the programmes we were forced, sometimes, to shorten poems because of the limits imposed by time. Here they are all given complete, except for the first poem, 'Puck's Song', where I have left off the last verse for aesthetic reasons, and the poem 'The English Flag' where only the first verse was relevant; and I have added in the second programme 'The Explanation' which we recorded and then were forced by time to cut out. The texts used throughout are those of the Definitive Edition of Kipling's Verse, published by Hodder and Stoughton.

Finally, I want to set on record my warmest thanks to the people who made the programmes possible: to Anthony Whitby, Controller of Radio Four who accepted the initial idea; to Helen Fry, the Producer, who insisted throughout on a standard of near-perfection that, through her, I believe we achieved; to her secretary, Vivian Gold, and to her assistant, Roger Thompson, not least because he found the ridiculously appropriate steam-organ version of 'Land of Hope and Glory' which introduced each pro-gramme; to the studio managers and recording staff, for whom no trouble seemed ever too great; and of course to the readers, without whom nothing, and especially to their patience in striving almost endlessly for the reading that was nearest to perfect.

I enjoyed making these programmes more than any other radio work I've done. I hope this book will share something of that pleasure with the people who read it.

Marghanita Laski

1 ROMAN BRITAIN TO THE NORMAN CONQUEST

All popular history is story-telling with a prejudice and, even when the prejudice isn't our own, we may still be captured by the way the story is told. What Rudyard Kipling's prejudices were is for you to discover. It's for his story-telling that I'm presenting some aspects of English history, as seen by Kipling in his verse.

Kipling was intoxicated by English history, and from earliest times till about 1821, there's hardly an important period or episode he didn't write a verse about. But, as with all poets who wrote easily and enormously, not everything Kipling wrote was good. He knew this himself, and he said that in all his best writing, his Daemon, as he called inspiration, took charge, and there was nothing left for the writer to do but to 'drift, wait and obey'. And even though it may mean some gaps in our history, I've hardly ever chosen a poem in which I didn't feel Kipling's Daemon took charge, or, at least, nudged his pen.

For Kipling, history and his modern world were inter-explanatory: each was to be understood in terms of the other. The British Empire reflects the Roman Empire. John Bunyan could interpret the Great War of 1914. All poems are, must be palimpsests, layers of meaning on layers of meaning, but, for Kipling, more directly, more immediately than most. At his best, Kipling could put on the skin of the man he was creating, no matter of what class or time, and especially when that man was of the kind he most respected and admired, which is to say, the responsible craftsman: the man who had mastered a skill – say, the skill of command, the skill of action, the skill of his hands, however simple – and who fully accepted the responsibilities of his skill. And because Kipling became the people he wrote about, we don't need to know much of Kipling himself. He was born in India in 1865, of middle-class creative parents. He was brought up in England, worked for seven years as a journalist in India, lived in America, in South Africa, and finally in Sussex, which is the heartland of some of his historical poems. He died in 1936.

We shall start Kipling's English History, as I think all popular history should start, by going backwards in time – here, backwards in Kipling's Sussex with 'Puck's Song':

[9]

See you the ferny ride that steals
Into the oak-woods far?
O that was whence they hewed the keels
That rolled to Trafalgar.

And mark you where the ivy clings
To Bayham's mouldering walls?
O there we cast the stout railings
That stand around St Paul's.

See you the dimpled track that runs
All hollow through the wheat?
O that was where they hauled the guns
That smote King Philip's fleet.

(Out of the Weald, the secret Weald,
Men sent in ancient years
The horse-shoes red at Flodden Field,
The arrows at Poitiers!)

See you our little mill that clacks,
So busy by the brook?
She has ground her corn and paid her tax
Ever since Domesday Book.

See you our stilly woods of oak,
And the dread ditch beside?
O that was where the Saxons broke
On the day that Harold died.

See you the windy levels spread
About the gates of Rye?
O that was where the Northmen fled,
When Alfred's ships came by.

See you our pastures wide and lone,
Where the red oxen browse?
O there was a City thronged and known,
Ere London boasted a house.

And see you, after rain, the trace
Of mound and ditch and wall?
O that was a Legion's camping-place,
When Caesar sailed from Gaul.

And see you marks that show and fade,
Like shadows on the Downs?
O they are the lines the Flint Men made,
To guard their wondrous towns.

Trackway and Camp and City lost,
Salt Marsh where now is corn –
Old Wars, old Peace, old Arts that cease,
And so was England born!

We are back now in England's past. We shall enter England's history with the Romans in Britain.

The Romans brought many things to this almost unknown barbarian country: fine buildings, great entertainment, central heating, the skills of writing and of law. It has been said that they brought roses and apple trees and pheasants. Certainly they brought many of the religions that pullulated through their vast empire, old religions like the worship of Jupiter, the new slave religion of the Christians, and, among the most influential, the soldier's religion, the worship of Mithras, originally a Persian God. This was a mystery religion, its shrines underground grottoes, its central rite the sacrificial slaying of a sacred bull by the young God, Mithras.

The worship of Mithras was strongest on the far-flung frontiers of the Roman Empire and it is on one such frontier, Hadrian's Wall in Northern Britain, that Kipling imagines a Roman soldier praying to his god:

A SONG TO MITHRAS   [*Voice: Gentry*]

Mithras, God of the Morning, our trumpets waken the Wall!
'Rome is above the Nations, but Thou art over all!'
Now as the names are answered, and the guards are marched away,
Mithras, also a soldier, give us strength for the day!

Roman relief of Mithras slaying the bull

Mithras, God of the Noontide, the heather swims in the heat.
Our helmets scorch our foreheads, our sandals burn our feet.
Now in the ungirt hour – now lest we blink and drowse,
Mithras, also a soldier, keep us true to our vows!

Mithras, God of the Sunset, low in the Western main –
Thou descending immortal, immortal to rise again!
Now when the watch is ended, now when the wine is drawn,
Mithras, also a soldier, keep us pure till the dawn!

Mithras, God of the Midnight, here where the great Bull dies,
Look on Thy children in darkness. Oh, take our sacrifice!
Many roads Thou hast fashioned – all of them lead to the Light!
Mithras, also a soldier, teach us to die aright!

Hadrian's Wall, where the soldier stood, was, for Rome, one of the frontiers between civilisation and barbarism. You can place that frontier anywhere, even inside yourself, but always on the other side there is the barbaric threat, and this is a part of what Kipling intended when he gave us a concrete civilisation, Rome, and on the other side a real enemy, the Picts, the little painted or tattooed people of the far north of Britain:

A PICT SONG   [*Voice: Northern Irish*]

Rome never looks where she treads.
    Always her heavy hooves fall
On our stomachs, our hearts or our heads;
    And Rome never heeds when we bawl.
Her sentries pass on – that is all,
    And we gather behind them in hordes,
And plot to reconquer the Wall,
    With only our tongues for our swords.

We are the Little Folk – we!
    Too little to love or to hate.
Leave us alone and you'll see

How we can drag down the State!
We are the worm in the wood!
We are the rot at the root!
We are the taint in the blood!
We are the thorn in the foot!

Mistletoe killing an oak –
Rats gnawing cables in two –
Moths making holes in a cloak –
How they must love what they do!
Yes – and we Little Folk too,
We are busy as they –
Working our works out of view –
Watch, and you'll see it some day!

No indeed! We are not strong,
But we know Peoples that are.
Yes, and we'll guide them along
To smash and destroy you in War!
We shall be slaves just the same?
Yes, we have always been slaves,
But you – you will die of the shame,
And then we shall dance on your graves!

We are the Little Folk – we!
Too little to love or to hate.
Leave us alone and you'll see
How we can drag down the State!
We are the worm in the wood!
We are the rot at the root!
We are the taint in the blood!
We are the thorn in the foot!

It was not only on Hadrian's Wall that the barbarians threatened, and the barbarians weren't only the Picts, but also the Goths and the Huns and the Vandals and the Visigoths, the Ostrogoths and the Franks, and not only the frontiers were threatened, but Rome herself. So round about the year 400 AD, from the distant outposts in distant Britain, the Legions were being called away.

The next poem, in the words of an old Roman centurion, is on a theme Kipling often returned to, the soldier sent to serve in foreign parts, and coming to love the land of his service more than the land of his birth:

THE ROMAN CENTURION'S SONG   [*Voice: North Country*]

Legate, I had the news last night – my cohort ordered home
By ship to Portus Itius and thence by road to Rome.
I've marched the companies aboard, the arms are stowed below:
Now let another take my sword. Command me not to go!

I've served in Britain forty years, from Vectis to the Wall.
I have none other home than this, nor any life at all.
Last night I did not understand, but, now the hour draws near
That calls me to my native land, I feel that land is here.

Here where men say my name was made, here where my work was done;
Here where my dearest dead are laid – my wife – my wife and son;
Here where time, custom, grief and toil, age, memory, service, love,
Have rooted me in British soil. Ah, how can I remove?

For me this land, that sea, these airs, those folk and fields suffice.
What purple Southern pomp can match our changeful Northern skies,
Black with December snows unshed or pearled with August haze –
The clanging arch of steel-grey March, or June's long-lighted days?

You'll follow widening Rhodanus till vine and olive lean
Aslant before the sunny breeze that sweeps Nemausus clean
To Arelate's triple gate; but let me linger on,
Here where our stiff-necked British oaks confront Euroclydon!

You'll take the old Aurelian Road through shore-descending pines
Where, blue as any peacock's neck, the Tyrrhene Ocean shines.
You'll go where laurel crowns are won, but – will you e'er forget
The scent of hawthorn in the sun, or bracken in the wet?

[16]

Roman mosaic floor from Low Ham, Somerset, showing scenes from Virgil

Let me work here for Britain's sake – at any task you will –
A marsh to drain, a road to make or native troops to drill.
Some Western camp (I know the Pict) or granite Border keep,
Mid seas of heather derelict, where our old messmates sleep.

Legate, I come to you in tears – My cohort ordered home!
I've served in Britain forty years. What should I do in Rome?
Here is my heart, my soul, my mind – the only life I know.
I cannot leave it all behind. Command me not to go!

But though, from all over the Empire, the Legions were recalled, they couldn't save Rome. In the year 410, Rome fell to the barbarians, and Kipling commemorates its fall with a jaunty marching song by a common soldier, a soldier who had served in Britain. The girl in the poem – just a soldier's girl – was called Lalage, I think because the Roman poet, Horace, wrote poems to a girl called Lalage, his sweetly-smiling, sweetly-speaking Lalage, and Kipling had a profound admiration for Horace. But our next isn't a Horatian poem. It's rather meant to be the Lili Marlene of its day:

'RIMINI'   [*Voice: Cockney*]

When I left Rome for Lalage's sake
By the Legions' Road to Rimini,
She vowed her heart was mine to take
With me and my shield to Rimini –
(Till the Eagles flew from Rimini –)
And I've tramped Britain, and I've tramped Gaul,
And the Pontic shore where the snow-flakes fall
As white as the neck of Lalage –
(As cold as the heart of Lalage!)
And I've lost Britain, and I've lost Gaul,
And I've lost Rome and, worst of all,
I've lost Lalage!

When you go by the Via Aurelia,
As thousands have travelled before,
Remember the Luck of the Soldier
Who never saw Rome any more!
Oh, dear was the sweetheart that kissed him,
And dear was the mother that bore;
But his shield was picked up in the heather
And he never saw Rome any more!

When you go by the Via Aurelia
That runs from the City to Gaul,
Remember the Luck of the Soldier
Who rose to be master of all!
He carried the sword and the buckler,
He mounted his guard on the Wall,
Till the Legions elected him Caesar,
And he rose to be master of all!

It's twenty-five marches to Narbo,
It's forty-five more up the Rhone,
And the end may be death in the heather
Or life on an Emperor's throne.
But whether the Eagles obey us,
Or we go to the Ravens – alone,
I'd sooner be Lalage's lover
Than sit on an Emperor's throne!

Rome lay sacked and desolate, and Britain was desolate too, in the mists of those Dark Ages of which we still know so little. The chroniclers tell of a king called Arthur and they tell of flying dragons too. It is certain that Britain was a power vacuum, as we now say, into which invaders poured. First, from

across the North Sea, came the Angles and Saxons and Jutes, who stayed to become the English, and, some of them, Christians. The Saxons of Kipling's Sussex were converted by St Wilfrid, who, although he came from North-umbria, stood, not for the old North British, the Celtic Christianity, but for the new Roman kind. In those days, there were many loving stories told about these early English priests and the animals they often saw as their brethren, and Kipling tells a story in this tradition, about Eddi, one of Wilfrid's Saxon priests:

EDDI'S SERVICE   [*Voice: Sussex*]

Eddi, priest of St Wilfrid
　　In his chapel at Manhood End,
Ordered a midnight service
　　For such as cared to attend.

But the Saxons were keeping Christmas,
　　And the night was stormy as well.
Nobody came to service,
　　Though Eddi rang the bell.

' 'Wicked weather for walking,'
　　Said Eddi of Manhood End.
'But I must go on with the service
　　For such as care to attend.'

The altar-lamps were lighted –
　　An old marsh-donkey came,
Bold as a guest invited,
　　And stared at the guttering flame.

The storm beat on at the windows,
　　The water splashed on the floor,
And a wet, yoke-weary bullock
　　Pushed in through the open door.

'How do I know what is greatest,
　　How do I know what is least?
That is My Father's business,'
　　Said Eddi, Wilfrid's priest.

'But – three are gathered together –
    Listen to me and attend.
I bring good news, my brethren!'
    Said Eddi of Manhood End.

And he told the Ox of a Manger
    And a Stall in Bethlehem,
And he spoke to the Ass of a Rider
    That rode to Jerusalem.

They steamed and dripped in the chancel,
    They listened and never stirred,
While, just as though they were Bishops,
    Eddi preached them The Word,

Till the gale blew off on the marshes
    And the windows showed the day,
And the Ox and the Ass together
    Wheeled and clattered away.

And when the Saxons mocked him,
    Said Eddi of Manhood End,
'I dare not shut His chapel
    On such as care to attend.'

Anglo-Saxon brooch, ninth century

Grotesque head English early twelfth century

A hundred years later, Britain was being ravaged by a new invader, the terrible Vikings, the Danes, who swept over the North Sea in their long ships each summer, leaving their women behind to wait, to work the farms, to bring up the children, to wait, surely resentfully, in the sheltered Scandinavian creeks.

HARP SONG OF THE DANE WOMEN   [*Voice: Orkney English*]

What is a woman that you forsake her,
And the hearth-fire and the home-acre,
To go with the old grey Widow-maker?

She has no house to lay a guest in –
But one chill bed for all to rest in,
That the pale suns and the stray bergs nest in.

She has no strong white arms to fold you,
But the ten-times-fingering weed to hold you –
Out on the rocks where the tide has rolled you.

Yet, when the signs of summer thicken,
And the ice breaks, and the birch-buds quicken,
Yearly you turn from our side, and sicken –

Sicken again for the shouts and the slaughters.
You steal away to the lapping waters,
And look at your ship in her winter-quarters.

You forget our mirth, and talk at the tables,
The kine in the shed and the horse in the stables –
To pitch her sides and go over her cables.

Then you drive out where the storm-clouds swallow,
And the sound of your oar-blades, falling hollow,
Is all we have left through the months to follow.

Ah, what is Woman that you forsake her,
And the hearth-fire and the home-acre,
To go with the old grey Widow-maker?

In the late ninth century, and especially under King Alfred, the English fought back, sometimes coming to terms with the Danes, sometimes even defeating them. But Alfred's successors were poorer timber, and, in 991, a new and shameful method was devised to deal with the Danes – devised, not surprisingly, by King Ethelred the Unready. To draw the moral, Kipling wrote, not, this time, poetry or even ballad, but simple verses, popular swinging verses of the kind by which perhaps he is best known:

DANE-GELD [*Voice: Gentry*]

It is always a temptation to an armed and agile nation
To call upon a neighbour and to say:—
'We invaded you last night – we are quite prepared to fight,
Unless you pay us cash to go away.'

And that is called asking for Dane-geld,
And the people who ask it explain
That you've only to pay 'em the Dane-geld
And then you'll get rid of the Dane!

It is always a temptation to a rich and lazy nation,
To puff and look important and to say:—
'Though we know we should defeat you, we have not the
    time to meet you.
We will therefore pay you cash to go away.'

And that is called paying the Dane-geld;
But we've proved it again and again,
That if once you have paid him the Dane-geld
You never get rid of the Dane.

It is wrong to put temptation in the path of any nation,
For fear they should succumb and go astray;
So when you are requested to pay up or be molested,
You will find it better policy to say:—

'We never pay *any*-one Dane-geld,
No matter how trifling the cost;
For the end of that game is oppression and shame,
And the nation that plays it is lost!'

I don't know if there's a moral in this too, but gradually the Danegeld turned into a perfectly respectable war tax. It was last collected by William the Conqueror, and it was to get the information needed to collect it efficiently that the Domesday Book record was made. We are up to the Conqueror now:

THE ANVIL [*Voice: Sussex*]

England's on the anvil – hear the hammers ring –
Clanging from the Severn to the Tyne!
Never was a blacksmith like our Norman King –
England's being hammered, hammered, hammered into line!

England's on the anvil! Heavy are the blows!
(But the work will be a marvel when it's done.)
Little bits of Kingdoms cannot stand against their foes.
England's being hammered, hammered, hammered into one!

There shall be one people – it shall serve one Lord –
(Neither Priest nor Baron shall escape!)
It shall have one speech and law, soul and strength and sword.
England's being hammered, hammered, hammered into shape!

The land-hungry Normans had come, and some of them stayed. Of one of them, Kipling wrote another of his poems about the soldier who served abroad and fell in love there:

SIR RICHARD'S SONG [*Voice: Gentry*]

I followed my Duke ere I was a lover,
To take from England fief and fee;
But now this game is the other way over –
But now England hath taken me!

I had my horse, my shield and banner,
And a boy's heart, so whole and free;
But now I sing in another manner –
But now England hath taken me!

As for my Father in his tower,
    Asking news of my ship at sea,
He will remember his own hour –
    Tell him England hath taken me!

As for my Mother in her bower,
    That rules my Father so cunningly,
She will remember a maiden's power –
    Tell her England hath taken me!

As for my Brother in Rouen City,
    A nimble and naughty page is he,
But he will come to suffer and pity –
    Tell him England hath taken me!

As for my little Sister waiting
    In the pleasant orchards of Normandie,
Tell her youth is the time for mating –
    Tell her England hath taken me!

As for my comrades in camp and highway,
    That lift their eyebrows scornfully,
Tell them their way is not my way –
    Tell them England hath taken me!

Kings and Princes and Barons famèd,
    Knights and Captains in your degree;
Hear me a little before I am blamèd –
    Seeing England hath taken me!

Howso great man's strength be reckoned,
    There are two things he cannot flee.
Love is the first, and Death is the second –
    And Love in England hath taken me!

For a long time after the Conquest the Normans were the bosses in England and the, by then, native Saxons were the serfs, the churls, the common men. The Norman masters spoke their own brand of French and they governed in that language. The Saxons spoke the primitive barbarian language that has become our English. It doesn't seem there was much love lost between conquerors and conquered, masters and servants, but perhaps some of the Norman barons felt as Kipling, in this next poem, thought it was proper for a Norman baron, or any other baron, to feel:

NORMAN AND SAXON   [*Voice: Southern English*]

'My son,' said the Norman Baron, 'I am dying, and you will be heir
To all the broad acres in England that William gave me for my share
When we conquered the Saxon at Hastings, and a nice little handful it is.
But before you go over to rule it I want you to understand this:—

'The Saxon is not like us Normans. His manners are not so polite.
But he never means anything serious till he talks about justice and right.
When he stands like an ox in the furrow with his sullen set eyes on your
    own,
And grumbles, "This isn't fair dealing," my son, leave the Saxon alone.

'You can horsewhip your Gascony archers, or torture your Picardy spears;
But don't try that game on the Saxon; you'll have the whole brood round
    your ears.
From the richest old Thane in the county to the poorest chained serf in the
    field,
They'll be at you and on you like hornets, and, if you are wise, you will
    yield.

'But first you must master their language, their dialect, proverbs and songs.
Don't trust any clerk to interpret when they come with the tale of their
    wrongs.
Let them know that you know what they're saying; let them feel that you
    know what to say.
Yes, even when you want to go hunting, hear 'em out if it takes you all
    day.

'They'll drink every hour of the daylight and poach every hour of the dark.
It's the sport not the rabbits they're after (we've plenty of game in the
    park).
Don't hang them or cut off their fingers. That's wasteful as well as unkind,
For a hard-bitten, South-country poacher makes the best man-at-arms you
    can find.

'Appear with your wife and the children at their weddings and funerals
    and feasts.
Be polite but not friendly to Bishops; be good to all poor parish priests.
Say "we", "us" and "ours" when you're talking, instead of "you fellows"
    and "I".
Don't ride over seeds; keep your temper; and *never you tell 'em a lie!*'

With Kipling, we've gone from the Romans, who came and went leaving
little behind but a few civilised words – *wine, bath, street,* indeed some streets
we still know, like Watling Street, and Icknield Way – and some ruins that
the Anglo-Saxons, who came next, called *enta geweorc,* the work of giants, and
fearfully avoided. The Danes have come and the Normans and now it won't
be Britain we're talking about any more, but England – England at the
opening of the Middle Ages.

Viking tombstone

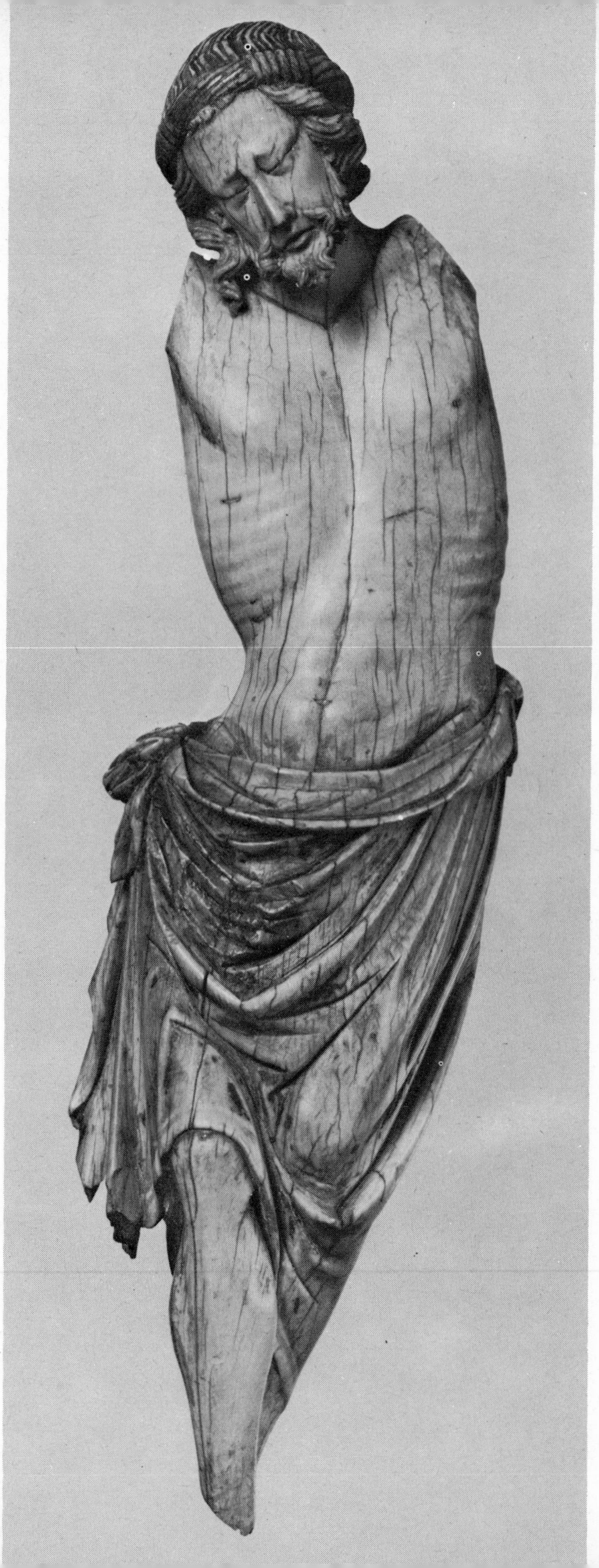

Fragment of an ivory crucifix. English fourteenth century

2 FROM THE MIDDLE AGES TO THE STUARTS

There is nothing in Rudyard Kipling's works that reveals his own religious position, and we don't need to know it, because with his phenomenal skill for entering the skins of men who engaged his sympathy, he could become, or nearly become, the Tibetan Lama of his story, *Kim* as he could become the Roman soldier who prayed to his god Mithras on Hadrian's Wall. And when Kipling wrote poems on England in the Middle Ages, which is roughly the period from the Norman Conquest till about 1500, he knew that medieval Christianity was the bedrock on which medieval poems must rest, even if they were, superficially, about something else.

But he knew too, that the Church was reft with internal dissension – it usually is – that on some men Christianity lay heavily, barred their way to what they felt might be a wider understanding; and that on other men Christianity lay, as the Church felt, too lightly. After all, Englishmen believed they were of classic pagan descent. They believed that Britain took its name from a certain Brutus, the son of Aeneas who fled from Troy and then came to England and gave London its first name of Troy Town. Maybe the English only half-believed this epic story, but certainly many of them still believed in the Old Religion, and perhaps they still do:

A TREE SONG   [*Voice: Southern English*]

> Of all the trees that grow so fair,
>   Old England to adorn,
> Greater are none beneath the Sun
>   Than Oak, and Ash, and Thorn.
> Sing Oak, and Ash, and Thorn, good sirs,
>   (All of a Midsummer morn!)
> Surely we sing no little thing
>   In Oak, and Ash, and Thorn!
>
> Oak of the Clay lived many a day
>   Or ever Aeneas began.
> Ash of the Loam was a lady at home
>   When Brut was an outlaw man.

Thorn of the Down saw New Troy Town
  (From which was London born);
Witness hereby the ancientry
  Of Oak, and Ash, and Thorn!

Yew that is old in churchyard-mould,
  He breedeth a mighty bow.
Alder for shoes do wise men choose,
  And beech for cups also.
But when ye have killed, and your bowl is spilled,
  And your shoes are clean outworn,
Back ye must speed for all that ye need
  To Oak, and Ash, and Thorn!

Ellum she hateth mankind, and waiteth
  Till every gust be laid
To drop a limb on the head of him
  That anyway trusts her shade.
But whether a lad be sober or sad,
  Or mellow with ale from the horn,
He will take no wrong when he lieth along
  'Neath Oak, and Ash, and Thorn!

Oh, do not tell the Priest our plight,
  Or he would call it a sin;
But – we have been out in the woods all night,
  A-conjuring Summer in!
And we bring you news by word of mouth –
  Good news for cattle and corn –
Now is the Sun come up from the South
  With Oak, and Ash, and Thorn!

Sing Oak, and Ash, and Thorn, good sirs
  (All of a Midsummer morn)!
England shall bide till Judgment Tide
  By Oak, and Ash, and Thorn!

Adoration of the magi, whalebone, English, twelfth century

But medieval Christianity had provided a cosmology, an explanation of the universe, and one that seemed, on the whole, to work; and an explanation, not only of the universe as a whole, the macrocosm, but also of the microcosm, Man. The next poem offers the medieval Christian explanation of one of man's abiding ills. We might call it ennui or boredom or depression. They called it Accidia or Wanhope, and they counted it as one of the Seven Deadly Sins. Kipling tells us how it assailed King Henry I's jester, Rahere, the founder of St Bartholomew's Hospital at Smithfield:

RAHERE   [*Voice: Gentry*]

Rahere, King Henry's Jester, feared by all the Norman Lords
For his eye that pierced their bosoms, for his tongue that shamed their
   swords;
Fed and flattered by the Churchmen – well they knew how deep he stood
In dark Henry's crooked counsels – fell upon an evil mood.

Suddenly, his days before him and behind him seemed to stand
Stripped and barren, fixed and fruitless, as those leagues of naked sand
When St Michael's ebb slinks outward to the bleak horizon-bound,
And the trampling wide-mouthed waters are withdrawn from sight and
   sound.

Then a Horror of Great Darkness sunk his spirit and, anon,
(Who had seen him wince and whiten as he turned to walk alone)
Followed Gilbert the Physician, and muttered in his ear,
'Thou hast it, O my brother?' 'Yea, I have it,' said Rahere.

'So it comes,' said Gilbert smoothly, 'man's most immanent distress.
'Tis a humour of the Spirit which abhorreth all excess;
And, whatever breed the surfeit – Wealth, or Wit, or Power, or Fame
(And thou hast each) the Spirit laboureth to expel the same.

'Hence the dulled eye's deep self-loathing – hence the loaded leaden brow;
Hence the burden of Wanhope that aches thy soul and body now.
Ay, the merriest fool must face it, and the wisest Doctor learn;
For it comes – it comes,' said Gilbert, 'as it passes – to return.'

[34]

But Rahere was in his torment, and he wandered, dumb and far,
Till he came to reeking Smithfield where the crowded gallows are,
(Followed Gilbert the Physician) and beneath the wry-necked dead,
Sat a leper and his woman, very merry, breaking bread.

He was cloaked from chin to ankle – faceless, fingerless, obscene –
Mere corruption swaddled man-wise, but the woman whole and clean;
And she waited on him crooning, and Rahere beheld the twain,
Each delighting in the other, and he checked and groaned again.

'So it comes, – it comes,' said Gilbert, 'as it came when Life began.
'Tis a motion of the Spirit that revealeth God to man.
In the shape of Love exceeding, which regards not taint or fall,
Since in perfect Love, saith Scripture, can be no excess at all.

'Hence the eye that sees no blemish – hence the hour that holds no shame.
Hence the Soul assured the Essence and the Substance are the same.
Nay, the meanest need not miss it, though the mightier pass it by;
For it comes – it comes,' said Gilbert, 'and, thou seest, it does not die!'

In the next poem, some critics have claimed to see Kipling's own religious position, and that a Christian one. I don't think they're right, but I don't understand the poem. It is called 'Cold Iron':

COLD IRON   [*Voice: Southern English*]

'Gold is for the mistress – silver for the maid –
Copper for the craftsman cunning at his trade.'
'Good!' said the Baron, sitting in his hall,
'But Iron – Cold Iron – is master of them all.'

So he made rebellion 'gainst the King his liege,
Camped before his citadel and summoned it to siege.
'Nay!' said the cannoneer on the castle wall,
'But Iron – Cold Iron – shall be master of you all!'

Woe for the Baron and his knights so strong,
When the cruel cannon-balls laid 'em all along;
He was taken prisoner, he was cast in thrall,
And Iron – Cold Iron – was master of it all!

Yet his King spake kindly (ah, how kind a Lord!)
'What if I release thee now and give thee back thy sword?'
'Nay!' said the Baron, 'mock not at my fall,
For Iron – Cold Iron – is master of men all.'

'Tears are for the craven, prayers are for the clown –
Halters for the silly neck that cannot keep a crown.'
'As my loss is grievous, so my hope is small,
For Iron – Cold Iron – must be master of men all!'

Yet his King made answer (few such Kings there be!)
'Here is Bread and here is Wine – sit and sup with me.
Eat and drink in Mary's Name, the whiles I do recall
How Iron – Cold Iron – can be master of men all!'

He took the Wine and blessed it. He blessed and brake the Bread,
With His own Hands He served Them, and presently He said:
'See! These Hands they pierced with nails, outside My city wall,
Show Iron – Cold Iron – to be master of men all.

[36]

'Wounds are for the desperate, blows are for the strong.
Balm and oil for weary hearts all cut and bruised with
   wrong.
I forgive thy treason – I redeem thy fall –
For Iron – Cold Iron – must be master of men all!'

'Crowns are for the valiant – sceptres for the bold!
Thrones and powers for mighty men who dare to take and hold.'
'Nay!' said the Baron, kneeling in his hall,
'But Iron – Cold Iron – is master of men all!
Iron out of Calvary is master of men all!'

In telling Kipling's English history, it is fair to use his pastiche verse, the verse he wrote in deliberate imitation of this or that poet or period. 'Gertrude's Prayer' was written for a short story, where, to hoodwink a wicked scholar, it's passed off as a poem by Chaucer. So we're giving it to you in Chaucerian English, that is, in the English that people were speaking in South-East England round about the year 1400, the English that had just superseded Norman-French as the language of Parliament and the Law Courts, and had become the language of the upper classes as well as the lower: the language, in short, of the English people:

GERTRUDE'S PRAYER   [*Voice: London Middle-English*]

That which is marred at birth Time shall not mend,
   Nor water out of bitter well make clean;
All evil thing returneth at the end,
   Or elseway walketh in our blood unseen.
Whereby the more is sorrow in certaine –
Dayspring mishandled cometh not againe.

To-bruizèd be that slender, sterting spray
   Out of the oake's rind that should betide
A branch of girt and goodliness, straightway
   Her spring is turnèd on herself, and wried
And knotted like some gall or veiney wen. –
Dayspring mishandled cometh not agen.

[37]

Noontide repayeth never morning-bliss –
    Sith noon to morn is incomparable;
And, so it be our dawning goth amiss,
    None other after-hour serveth well.
Ah! Jesu-Moder, pitie my oe paine –
Dayspring mishandled cometh not againe!

Chaucer was a Londoner, and it was the language of that region that became our Gentry English and our Cockney of today. But in the late Middle Ages, the other regional languages still had great strength, and so had regional poetry; especially, in the North, the ballad poetry. Kipling's next poem is an authentic North-Country late-medieval ballad – authentic in everything but in being written by a Southerner near to our own times. It's called 'Heriot's Ford'.

HERIOT'S FORD   [*Voice: North Country*]

'What's that that hirples at my side?'
The foe that you must fight, my lord.
'That rides as fast as I can ride?'
The shadow of your might, my lord.

'Then wheel my horse against the foe!'
He's down and overpast, my lord.
You war against the sunset-glow,
The judgment follows fast, my lord!

'Oh, who will stay the sun's descent?'
King Joshua he is dead, my lord.
'I need an hour to repent!'
'Tis what our sister said, my lord.

'Oh, do not slay me in my sins!'
You're safe awhile with us, my lord.
'Nay, kill me ere my fear begins!'
We would not serve you thus, my lord.

'Where is the doom that I must face?'
Three little leagues away, my lord.
'Then mend the horses' laggard pace!'
We need them for next day, my lord.

'Next day – next day! Unloose my cords!'
Our sister needed none, my lord.
You had no mind to face our swords,
And – where can cowards run, my lord?

'You would not kill the soul alive?'
'Twas thus our sister cried, my lord.
'I dare not die with none to shrive.'
But so our sister died, my lord.

'Then wipe the sweat from brow and cheek.'
It runnels forth afresh, my lord.
'Uphold me – for the flesh is weak.'
You've finished with the Flesh, my lord!

A ballad like 'Heriot's Ford' might still turn up in the North of England. But by the end of the fifteenth century, in Southern England at least, the light of the Renaissance was breaking. For Kipling, dawn, and the wind that gets up just before dawn, were often his moment of inspiration, when a creative idea broke through. So this is the image that he chose to symbolise that moment of new birth in history, the Renaissance:

THE DAWN WIND   [*Voice: Sussex*]

At two o'clock in the morning, if you open your window and listen,
You will hear the feet of the Wind that is going to call the sun.
And the trees in the shadow rustle and the trees in the moonlight glisten,
And though it is deep, dark night, you feel that the night is done.

So do the cows in the field. They graze for an hour and lie down,
Dozing and chewing the cud; or a bird in the ivy wakes,
Chirrups one note and is still, and the restless Wind strays on,
Fidgeting far down the road, till, softly, the darkness breaks.

Back comes the Wind full strength with a blow like an angel's wing,
Gentle but waking the world, as he shouts: 'The Sun! The Sun!'
And the light floods over the fields and the birds begin to sing,
And the Wind dies down in the grass. It is day and his work is done.

So when the world is asleep, and there seems no hope of her waking
Out of some long, bad dream that makes her mutter and moan,
Suddenly, all men arise to the noise of fetters breaking,
And every one smiles at his neighbour and tells him his soul is his own!

The Renaissance, as we all know, brought to England the new learning of
Europe, and with it the new poetry, the poetry of intricately rhyming
patterns that now, finally, took over from the old alliterative verse. In early
Tudor England the poets were experimenting beautifully in this new verse.
The Elizabethan Age saw its flowering. It flowered into the clever, con-
ceited, convoluted verse of the lighter poets – Lodge, Peel, Greene, Lyly –
and Kipling's pastiche 'The Explanation' could pass for an epigrammatic
lyric by any of these:

THE EXPLANATION   [*Voice: Gentry*]

Love and Death once ceased their strife
At the Tavern of Man's Life.
Called for wine, and threw – alas!
Each his quiver on the grass.
When the bout was o'er they found
Mingled arrows strewed the ground.
Hastily they gathered then
Each the loves and lives of men.
Ah, the fateful dawn deceived!
Mingled arrows each one sheaved.
Death's dread armoury was stored
With the shafts he most abhorred;
Love's light quiver groaned beneath
Venom-headed darts of Death.

Thus it was they wrought our woe
At the Tavern long ago.
Tell me, do our masters know,
Loosing blindly as they fly,
Old men love while young men die?

Another flowering of this Renaissance poetry in England was into the more serious metaphysical poetry of writers like John Donne. This was a strain Kipling often worked in. He used it for a poem about the young Elizabethans, who, while England maintained precarious peace with Spain, fought and raided for England as pirates, dishonoured and disowned if they were caught, but ready to risk life and honour for the great Queen whom they worshipped – it isn't too strong a word – under such titles as Cynthia, Gloriana, Belphœbe:

THE QUEEN'S MEN   [*Voice: Gentry*]

Valour and Innocence
Have latterly gone hence
To certain death by certain shame attended.
Envy – ah! even to tears! –
The fortune of their years
Which, though so few, yet so divinely ended.

Scarce had they lifted up
Life's full and fiery cup,
Than they had set it down untouched before them.
Before their day arose
They beckoned it to close –
Close in confusion and destruction o'er them.

They did not stay to ask
What prize should crown their task –
Well sure that prize was such as no man strives for;
But passed into eclipse,
Her kiss upon their lips –
Even Belphœbe's, whom they gave their lives for!

Belphœbe, the beautiful moon – all very well for a young radiant queen, surrounded by adoring, or apparently adoring young courtiers, but even queens grow old. The next poem is in the form of a country dance:

THE LOOKING-GLASS   [*Voices: Gentry and Southern English*]

Queen Bess was Harry's daughter. Stand forward partners all!

The Queen was in her chamber, and she was middling old.
Her petticoat was satin, and her stomacher was gold.
Backwards and forwards and sideways did she pass,
Making up her mind to face the cruel looking-glass.
The cruel looking-glass that will never show a lass
As comely or as kindly or as young as what she was!

Queen Bess was Harry's daughter. Now hand your partners all!

The Queen was in her chamber, a-combing of her hair.
There came Queen Mary's spirit and It stood behind her chair,
Singing 'Backwards and forwards and sideways may you pass,
But I will stand behind you till you face the looking-glass.
The cruel looking-glass that will never show a lass
As lovely or unlucky or as lonely as I was!'

Queen Bess was Harry's daughter. Now turn your partners all!

The Queen was in her chamber, a-weeping very sore,
There came Lord Leicester's spirit and It scratched upon the door,
Singing 'Backwards and forwards and sideways may you pass,
But I will walk beside you till you face the looking-glass.
The cruel looking-glass that will never show a lass,
As hard and unforgiving or as wicked as you was!'

Queen Bess was Harry's daughter. Now kiss your partners all!

The Queen was in her chamber, her sins were on her head.
She looked the spirits up and down and statelily she said:—
'Backwards and forwards and sideways though I've been,
Yet I am Harry's daughter and I am England's Queen!'

And she faced the looking-glass (and whatever else there was)
And she saw her day was over and she saw her beauty pass
In the cruel looking-glass, that can always hurt a lass
More hard than any ghost there is or any man there was!

In 1603 Queen Elizabeth died. Her successor was James Stuart, James VI of Scotland, James I of England, the man whom his brother-King, King Henry IV of France, Henry of Navarre, called 'The wisest fool in Christendom':

JAMES I   [*Voice: Gentry*]

The child of Mary Queen of Scots,
   A shifty mother's shiftless son,
Bred up among intrigues and plots,
   Learnèd in all things, wise in none.
Ungainly, babbling, wasteful, weak,
   Shrewd, clever, cowardly, pedantic,
The sight of steel would blanch his cheek
   The smell of baccy drive him frantic.
He was the author of his line –
   He wrote that witches should be burnt;
He wrote that monarchs were divine,
   And left a son who – proved they weren't!

I believe we tend to think of Shakespeare as an Elizabethan, and it's true that his earlier plays were performed in Queen Elizabeth's reign; it's said that *The Merry Wives of Windsor* was written by order of the Queen herself. But many of his greatest plays were written in the reign of James I: *Othello, Lear, Macbeth,* and of course, *The Tempest.* Our next poem is about *The Tempest,* but it also reminds us of the wealth that the voyages of the English nation brought to England: not only the gold of the New World (and never so much of that as King James I wanted), not only new plants and spices and unguents, tobacco and potatoes, strange swarthy men, and women like the beautiful Indian Princess Pocahontas, but also tales, marvellous tales:

TERRARUM TYPUS DE INTEGRO

ASIA

AMERICA

Polus Arcticus

Circulus Arcticus

Anian

AMERICA

1492 Christophor. Columbo nomine Regis

MEXICANA

Zubgara

NOVA FRANCIA

Chilaga

Avanares

Avacal

CALIFORNIA

AMERICA

Florida

Golfo Mexicano

Tropicus Canceri

MAR DEL NORT

MAR DEL ZUR

Circulus Aequinoctialis

Oceanus Peruvianus

PERU

Amazones

BRASILIA

Tropicus Capricorni

EL MAR PACIFICO

THE COINER   [*Voice: North Country*]

Against the Bermudas we foundered, whereby
This Master, that Swabber, yon Bo'sun, and I
(Our pinnace and crew being drowned in the main)
Must beg for our bread through old England again.

For a bite and a sup, and a bed of clean straw,
We'll tell you such marvels as man never saw,
On a Magical Island which no one did spy
Save this Master, that Swabber, yon Bo'sun, and I.

Seven months among Mermaids and Devils and Sprites,
And Voices that howl in the cedars o' nights,
With further enchantments we underwent there.
Good Sirs, 'tis a tale to draw guts from a bear!

'Twixt Dover and Southwark it paid us our way,
Where we found some poor players were labouring a play;
And, willing to search what such business might be,
We entered the yard, both to hear and to see.

One hailed us for seamen and courteous-ly
Did guide us apart to a tavern near by
Where we told him our tale (as to many of late),
And he gave us good cheer, so we gave him good weight.

Mulled sack and strong waters on bellies well lined
With beef and black pudding do strengthen the mind;
And seeing him greedy for marvels, at last
From plain salted truth to flat leasing we passed.

But he, when on midnight our reckoning he paid,
Says, 'Never match coins with a Coiner by trade,
Or he'll turn your lead pieces to metal as rare
As shall fill him this globe, and leave something to spare. . . .'

We slept where they laid us, and when we awoke
'Was a crown or five shillings in every man's poke.
We bit them and rang them, and, finding them good,

We drank to that Coiner as honest men should!

For a cup and a crust, and a truss of clean straw,
We'll tell you such marvels as man never saw.

The Tempest was first performed in 1611. It was Shakespeare's last play, and after it he returned to Stratford, where he died in 1616. Kipling's poem, 'The Craftsman', is, I think, one of his finest; it's about Shakespeare talking to Ben Jonson, perhaps on one of his visits to London we know he made after his retirement, talking till late into the night at the Mermaid Tavern in Bread Street:

THE CRAFTSMAN [*Voice: Southern English*]

Once, after long-drawn revel at The Mermaid,
He to the overbearing Boanerges
Jonson, uttered (if half of it were liquor,
          Blessed be the vintage!)

Saying how, at an alehouse under Cotswold,
He had made sure of his very Cleopatra,
Drunk with enormous, salvation-contemning
          Love for a tinker.

How, while he hid from Sir Thomas's keepers,
Crouched in a ditch and drenched by the midnight
Dews, he had listened to gipsy Juliet
          Rail at the dawning.

How at Bankside, a boy drowning kittens
Winced at the business; whereupon his sister –
Lady Macbeth aged seven – thrust 'em under,
          Sombrely scornful.

How on a Sabbath, hushed and compassionate –
She being known since her birth to the townsfolk –
Stratford dredged and delivered from Avon
          Dripping Ophelia.

So, with a thin third finger marrying
Drop to wine-drop domed on the table,
Shakespeare opened his heart till the sunrise –
Entered to hear him.

London wakened and he, imperturbable,
Passed from waking to hurry after shadows . . .
Busied upon shows of no earthly importance?
Yes, but he knew it!

Sturt Sculp.

Frontispiece from an edition of 'Pilgrim's Progress' of 1728

3 FROM THE CIVIL WAR TO THE DEATH OF NAPOLEON

I was in the Kremlin a few years ago looking at a fine collection of seventeenth-century silver. The guide said, 'That's all English. It was sold to us during one of your bourgeois revolutions.'

What the girl dismissed so casually was, in fact, the English Revolution of 1642 to 1660, the event that, perhaps more than any other in our history, moves the popular historians of today. They see it as the forerunner of all subsequent European Peoples' Revolutions, including, as I told the guide, the Russian Revolution of 1917. And what perhaps most distinguishes Rudyard Kipling from later popular historians is that this English Revolution seems hardly to have moved him at all. Clashes of principle he could understand, but popular movements he profoundly distrusted. To him, a well-governed country was one in which skilled responsible individuals of all classes worked together, each in his own craft, for the common good, and carried the burden of the unskilled and the irresponsible. Kipling could understand the individual who got out and away because his country or its outlook was too small for him or got too hot to hold him, but he had no sympathy for the man who stayed there and tried to pull down the state.

So the English Revolution, or, as we usually call it, the Civil War, seems to have found him at a loss. Whether his sympathies lay with the Royalists who sold their silver plate to pay for their cause, or with the Parliamentarians and the many sets of levellers who stood more or less at their side, we don't know. He wrote only one poem on the Civil War – on the Battle of Edgehill of 1642 which opened that War and which, though Charles I's forces claimed the victory, was, in fact, something near a draw:

EDGEHILL FIGHT   [*Voice: Southern English*]

> Naked and grey the Cotswolds stand
>   Beneath the autumn sun,
> And the stubble-fields on either hand
>   Where Stour and Avon run.
> There is no change in the patient land
>   That has bred us every one.

She should have passed in cloud and fire
   And saved us from this sin
Of war – red war – 'twixt child and sire,
   Household and kith and kin,
In the heart of a sleepy Midland shire,
   With the harvest scarcely in.

But there is no change as we meet at last
   On the brow-head or the plain,
And the raw astonished ranks stand fast
   To slay or to be slain
By the men they knew in the kindly past
   That shall never come again –

By the men they met at dance or chase,
   In the tavern or the hall,
At the justice-bench and the market-place,
   At the cudgel-play or brawl –
Of their own blood and speech and race,
   Comrades or neighbours all!

More bitter than death this day must prove
   Whichever way it go,
For the brothers of the maids we love
   Make ready to lay low
Their sisters' sweethearts, as we move
   Against our dearest foe.

Thank Heaven! At last the trumpets peal
   Before our strength gives way.
For King or for the Commonweal –
   No matter which they say,
The first dry rattle of new-drawn steel
   Changes the world to-day!

Kipling was, of course, right. The world *was* changed. It always is. And it was changed, not only by the victors who established the sovereignty of Parliament, never again to be wholly lost. England was also changed by the losers. For many of those on the side of Church and King had spent the years of the Commonwealth abroad. Some of them were scholars and natural philosophers: what we should now call scientists. Some of them were virtuosi: what we should call connoisseurs of the arts. And when they came back after the Restoration of 1660, once again new learning from Europe came with them.

We often forget that the early years of the Restoration as much as the early years of the Commonwealth looked like a dawn in which it was bliss to be alive. But the high hopes were blasted, as over-high hopes usually are, and at Charles II's court dissipation, extravagance, and sloth took over. Samuel Pepys in those days was Secretary to the Admiralty, one of our great public servants who did all he could to ensure that our Navy was in fighting trim against the Dutch. But it wasn't. And the English sailors knew why:

THE DUTCH IN THE MEDWAY   [*Voice: Cockney*]

If wars were won by feasting,
   Or victory by song,
Or safety found in sleeping sound,
   How England would be strong!
But honour and dominion
   Are not maintainèd so.
They're only got by sword and shot,
   And this the Dutchmen know!

The moneys that should feed us
   You spend on your delight,
How can you then have sailor-men
   To aid you in your fight?
Our fish and cheese are rotten,
   Which makes the scurvy grow –
We cannot serve you if we starve,
   And this the Dutchmen know!

[53]

Our ships in every harbour
    Be neither whole nor sound,
And, when we seek to mend a leak,
    No oakum can be found;
Or, if it is, the caulkers,
    And carpenters also,
For lack of pay have gone away,
    And this the Dutchmen know!

Mere powder, guns, and bullets,
    We scarce can get at all;
Their price was spent in merriment
    And revel at Whitehall,

The Dutch in the Medway, 1667

While we in tattered doublets
    From ship to ship must row,
Beseeching friends for odds and ends –
    And this the Dutchmen know!

No King will heed our warnings,
    No Court will pay our claims –
Our King and Court for their desport
    Do sell the very Thames!
For, now De Ruyter's topsails
    Off naked Chatham show,
We dare not meet him with our fleet –
    And this the Dutchmen know!

The topsails of De Ruyter's Dutch Fleet were seen in Chatham for three days in the June of 1667. Contemptuously the Dutch had sailed up the Medway, burnt a few of our ships, captured a flag-ship and sailed away again. But if politically a shameful period, the Restoration was also a creative one, and not only in science and poetry and music and the jolly bawdy plays we know as Restoration Drama. Not all the Puritans had vanished with the Restoration and one of these Puritans, a man who had fought in the Parliamentary Army, was the author of *Pilgrim's Progress*, published in 1678. Four years later he wrote another book called *The Holy War*. Kipling, writing during the Great War, saw these two wars as one:

THE HOLY WAR   [*Voice: Bedfordshire*]

A tinker out of Bedford,
*   A vagrant oft in quod,*
A private under Fairfax,
*   A minister of God –*
Two hundred years and thirty
*   Ere Armageddon came*
His single hand portrayed it,
*   And Bunyan was his name!*

He mapped for those who follow,
    The world in which we are –
'This famous town of Mansoul'
    That takes the Holy War.
Her true and traitor people,
    The Gates along her wall,
From Eye Gate unto Feel Gate,
    John Bunyan showed them all.

All enemy divisions,
    Recruits of every class,
And highly screened positions
    For flame or poison-gas;
The craft that we call modern,
    The crimes that we call new,

John Bunyan had 'em typed and filed
    In Sixteen Eighty-two.

Likewise the Lords of Looseness
    That hamper faith and works,
The Perseverance-Doubters,
    And Present-Comfort shirks,
With brittle intellectuals
    Who crack beneath a strain –
John Bunyan met that helpful set
    In Charles the Second's reign.

Emmanuel's vanguard dying
    For right and not for rights,
My Lord Appollyon lying
    To the State-kept Stockholmites,
The Pope, the swithering Neutrals,
    The Kaiser and his Gott –
Their rôles, their goals, their naked souls –
    He knew and drew the lot.

Now he hath left his quarters,
    In Bunhill Fields to lie,
The wisdom that he taught us
    Is proven prophecy –
One watchword through our Armies,
    One answer from our Lands:—
'No dealings with Diabolus
    As long as Mansoul stands!'

A pedlar from a hovel,
    The lowest of the low –
The Father of the Novel,
    Salvation's first Defoe –
Eight blinded generations
    Ere Armageddon came,
He showed us how to meet it,
    And Bunyan was his name!

One thing the English have never been able to do successfully is to rule the Celts, and least of all the Irish. In the twelfth century, under Henry II, the ruffian baron, Strongbow, conquered, but failed to rule. Brutal colonisation under Tudors and Stuarts, and then Cromwell's land settlement left the Irish helpless serfs in their own land. Many of the toughest got out and went abroad, some to make new peaceful lives there, but some to fight more effectively against the hated English. These were the famous Wild Geese of Irish history. In 1740 the War of the Austrian Succession broke out, and when the English were defeated at Fontenoy in Belgium by the French under Marshal Saxe, fighting with the French was an Irish Brigade of these same 'Wild Geese':

THE IRISH GUARDS　　　[*Voice: Southern Irish*]

We're not so old in the Army List,
　　But we're not so young at our trade,
For we had the honour at Fontenoy
　　Of meeting the Guards' Brigade.
'Twas Lally, Dillon, Bulkeley, Clare,
　　And Lee that led us then,
And after a hundred and seventy years
　　We're fighting for France again!
　　Old Days! The wild geese are flighting,
　　　Head to the storm as they faced it before!
　　For where there are Irish there's bound to be fighting,
　　　And when there's no fighting, it's Ireland no more!
　　　　　　　Ireland no more!

The fashion's all for khaki now,
　　But once through France we went
Full-dressed in scarlet Army cloth
　　The English – left at Ghent.
They're fighting on our side to-day
　　But, before they changed their clothes,
The half of Europe knew our fame,
　　As all of Ireland knows!

[58]

Old Days! The wild geese are flying,
Head to the storm as they faced it before!
For where there are Irish there's memory undying,
And when we forget, it is Ireland no more!
Ireland no more!

From Barry Wood to Gouzeaucourt,
From Boyne to Pilkem Ridge,
The ancient days come back no more
Than water under the bridge.
But the bridge it stands and the water runs
As red as yesterday,
And the Irish move to the sound of the guns
Like salmon to the sea.
Old Days! The wild geese are ranging,
Head to the storm as they faced it before!
For where there are Irish their hearts are unchanging,
And when they are changed, it is Ireland no more!
Ireland no more!

We're not so old in the Army List,
But we're not so new in the ring,
For we carried our packs with Marshal Saxe
When Louis was our King.
But Douglas Haig's our Marshal now
And we're King George's men,
And after one hundred and seventy years
We're fighting for France again!
Ah, France! And did we stand by you,
When life was made splendid with gifts and rewards?
Ah, France! And will we deny you
In the hour of your agony, Mother of Swords?
Old Days! The wild geese are flighting,
Head to the storm as they faced it before!
For where there are Irish there's loving and fighting,
And when we stop either, it's Ireland no more!
Ireland no more!

I've said that Kipling disapproved of rebellions in general, but one rebellion against British rule he saw as a natural evolution in the history of two great sister nations. This was the American Rebellion, as he called it, the American War of Independence which erupted in 1773 after the famous Boston Tea Party. In 1777 to 1778, General George Washington set up the winter quarters of his army in a small village in Pennsylvania called Valley Forge. It was Valley Forge that Kipling chose to commemorate when looking back on that rebellion:

THE AMERICAN REBELLION: AFTER   [*Voice: New-England English*]

The snow lies thick on Valley Forge,
    The ice on the Delaware,
But the poor dead soldiers of King George
    They neither know nor care.

Not though the earliest primrose break
    On the sunny side of the lane,
And scuffling rookeries awake
    Their England's spring again.

They will not stir when the drifts are gone,
    Or the ice melts out of the bay:
And the men that served with Washington
    Lie all as still as they.

They will not stir though the mayflower blows
    In the moist dark woods of pine,
And every rock-strewn pasture shows
    Mullein and columbine.

Each for his land, in a fair fight,
    Encountered, strove, and died,
And the kindly earth that knows no spite
    Covers them side by side.

She is too busy to think of war;
    She has all the world to make gay;
And, behold, the yearly flowers are
    Where they were in our fathers' day!

Golden-rod by the pasture-wall
When the columbine is dead,
And sumach leaves that turn, in fall,
Bright as the blood they shed.

After the British surrender at Yorktown, the victorious Americans set up their capital in Philadelphia, the city of brotherly love founded by the Quaker, William Penn, as a place where men might freely follow their own beliefs. By the 1790s, European refugees of all kinds had long been coming to Philadelphia. Count Zinzendorf, banished from Saxony, had found freedom for his Moravian Church there. And there Talleyrand, banished from revolutionary France, eked out a precarious living. In fact, almost every reference in Kipling's poem 'Philadelphia' is to a real person and a real place:

PHILADELPHIA   [*Voice: New-England English*]

If you're off to Philadelphia in the morning,
You mustn't take my stories for a guide.
There's little left, indeed, of the city you will read of,
And all the folk I write about have died.

Now few will understand if you mention Talleyrand,
Or remember what his cunning and his skill did;
And the cabmen at the wharf do not know Count Zinzendorf,
Nor the Church in Philadelphia he builded.

It is gone, gone, gone with lost Atlantis,
(Never say I didn't give you warning).
In Seventeen Ninety-three 'twas there for all to see,
But it's not in Philadelphia this morning.

If you're off to Philadelphia in the morning,
You mustn't go by anything I've said.
Bob Bicknell's Southern Stages have been laid aside for ages,

But the Limited will take you there instead.
Toby Hirte can't be seen at One Hundred and Eighteen
North Second Street – no matter when you call;
And I fear you'll search in vain for the wash-house
    down the lane
Where Pharoah played the fiddle at the ball.

It is gone, gone, gone with Thebes the Golden,
(Never say I didn't give you warning).
In Seventeen Ninety-four 'twas a famous dancing floor –
But it's not in Philadelphia this morning.

If you're off to Philadelphia in the morning,
You must telegraph for rooms at some Hotel.
You needn't try your luck at Epply's or 'The Buck,'
Though the Father of his Country liked them well.
It is not the slightest use to inquire for Adam Goos,
Or to ask where Pastor Meder has removed – so
You must treat as out of date the story I relate
Of the Church in Philadelphia he loved so.

He is gone, gone, gone with Martin Luther
(Never say I didn't give you warning).
In Seventeen Ninety-five he was (rest his soul!) alive,
But he's not in Philadelphia this morning.

If you're off to Philadelphia this morning,
And wish to prove the truth of what I say,
I pledge my word you'll find the pleasant land behind
Unaltered since Red Jacket rode that way.
Still the pine-woods scent the noon; still the catbird
    sings his tune;
Still autumn sets the maple-forest blazing;
Still the grape-vine through the dusk flings her
    soul-compelling musk;
Still the fire-flies in the corn make night amazing!

They are there, there, there with Earth immortal
(Citizens, I give you friendly warning).
The things that truly last when men and times
   have passed,
They are all in Pennsylvania this morning!

And Count Zinzendorf's Moravian Church is this very morning still standing in Philadelphia.

   First the English Revolution, next the American Revolution, and then, in 1789, the French Revolution, supported by the Americans, terrifying to most of the English. But the French Revolutionary wars and the Napoleonic Wars that followed were welcomed by the smugglers, French and British alike:

'POOR HONEST MEN'   [*Voice: Southern English*]

Your jar of Virginny
Will cost you a guinea,
Which you reckon too much by five shillings or ten;
But light your churchwarden
And judge it according,
When I've told you the troubles of poor honest men.

From the Capes of the Delaware,
As you are well aware,
We sail with tobacco for England – but then,
Our own British cruisers,
They watch us come through, sirs,
And they press half a score of us poor honest men!

Or if by quick sailing
(Thick weather prevailing)
We leave them behind (as we do now and then)
We are sure of a gun from
Each frigate we run from,
Which is often destruction to poor honest men!

Broadsides the Atlantic
We tumble short-handed,

[64]

With shot-holes to plug and new canvas to bend;
And off the Azores,
Dutch, Dons and Monsieurs
Are waiting to terrify poor honest men.

Napoleon's embargo
Is laid on all cargo
Which comfort or aid to King George may intend;
And since roll, twist and leaf,
Of all comforts is chief,
They try for to steal it from poor honest men!

With no heart for fight,
We take refuge in flight,
But fire as we run, our retreat to defend;
Until our stern-chasers
Cut up her fore-braces,
And she flies off the wind from us poor honest men!

'Twix' the Forties and Fifties,
South-eastward the drift is,
And so, when we think we are making Land's End,
Alas, it is Ushant
With half the King's Navy,
Blockading French ports against poor honest men!

But they may not quit station
(Which is our salvation)
So swiftly we stand to the Nor'ard again;
And finding the tail of
A homeward-bound convoy,
We slip past the Scillies like poor honest men.

'Twix' the Lizard and Dover,
We hand our stuff over,
Though I may not inform how we do it, nor when.
But a light on each quarter,
Low down on the water,
Is well understood by poor honest men.

Even then we have dangers,
From meddlesome strangers,
Who spy on our business and are not content
To take a smooth answer,
Except with a handspike . . .
And they say they are murdered by poor honest men!

To be drowned or be shot
Is our natural lot,
Why should we, moreover, be hanged in the end –
After all our great pains
For to dangle in chains
As though we were smugglers, not poor honest men?

The smuggled goods have been secretly landed and the land smugglers, the
Gentlemen, take over. In the coastal counties of Southern England there
was hardly a family that hadn't a finger in the trade:

A SMUGGLER'S SONG   [*Voice: West Country*]

If you wake at midnight, and hear a horse's feet,
Don't go drawing back the blind, or looking in the street,
Them that asks no questions isn't told a lie.
Watch the wall, my darling, while the Gentlemen go by!
 Five and twenty ponies
 Trotting through the dark –
 Brandy for the Parson,
 'Baccy for the Clerk;
 Laces for a lady, letters for a spy,
And watch the wall, my darling, while the Gentlemen go by!

Running round the woodlump if you chance to find
Little barrels, roped and tarred, all full of brandy-wine,
Don't you shout to come and look, nor use 'em for your play.
Put the brishwood back again – and they'll be gone next day!

Seventeenth-century French lace

If you see the stable-door setting open wide;
If you see a tired horse lying down inside;
If your mother mends a coat cut about and tore;
If the lining's wet and warm – don't you ask no more!

If you meet King George's men, dressed in blue and red,
You be careful what you say, and mindful what is said.
If they call you 'pretty maid', and chuck you 'neath the chin,
Don't you tell where no one is, nor yet where no one's been!

Knocks and footsteps round the house – whistles after dark –
You've no call for running out till the house-dogs bark.
Trusty's here, and *Pincher's* here, and see how dumb they lie –
They don't fret to follow when the Gentlemen go by!

If you do as you've been told, 'likely there's a chance,
You'll be give a dainty doll, all the way from France,
With a cap of Valenciennes, and a velvet hood –
A present from the Gentlemen, along o' being good!
   Five and twenty ponies
   Trotting through the dark –
   Brandy for the Parson,
   'Baccy for the Clerk.
Them that asks no questions isn't told a lie –
Watch the wall, my darling, while the Gentlemen go by!

But in the early 1800s not everyone was concerned with the war. It went on, after all, with only a brief respite, from 1793 till Waterloo in 1815, and life had to be lived. It's well known that Jane Austen, with two brothers in the Navy, ignored the war in her novels. Jane Austen died in 1817, and Kipling, who greatly admired her work, wrote a loving but, I'm afraid, sadly in-accurate poem about her entry into Heaven where she is introduced by Sir Walter Scott, and welcomed by Fielding and by Smollett and by the author of Don Quixote:

Jane went to Paradise:
    That was only fair.
Good Sir Walter followed her,
    And armed her up the stair.
Henry and Tobias,
    And Miguel of Spain,
Stood with Shakespeare at the top
    To welcome Jane –

Then the Three Archangels
    Offered out of hand
Anything in Heaven's gift
    That she might command.
Azrael's eyes upon her,
    Raphael's wings above,
Michael's sword against her heart,
    Jane said: 'Love.'

Instantly the under-
    standing Seraphim
Laid their fingers on their lips
    And went to look for him.
Stole across the Zodiac,
    Harnessed Charles's Wain,
And whispered round the Nebulæ
    'Who loved Jane?'

In a private limbo
    Where none had thought to look,
Sat a Hampshire gentleman
    Reading of a book.
It was called *Persuasion*,
    And it told the plain
Story of the love between
    Him and Jane.

He heard the question
    Circle Heaven through –
Closed the book and answered:
    'I did – and do!'
Quietly but speedily
    (As Captain Wentworth moved)
Entered into Paradise
    The man Jane loved!

Jane lies in Winchester, blessèd be her shade!
Praise the Lord for making her, and her for all she made.
And, while the stones of Winchester – or Milsom Street – remain,
Glory, Love, and Honour unto England's Jane!

In 1821, on the island of St Helena in the South Atlantic, there died the Ogre, the Corsican Monster, Napoleon Bonaparte. On Napoleon's death, Kipling wrote 'A St Helena Lullaby':

A ST HELENA LULLABY
[*Voices: West Country – the questions in a child's voice*]

'How far is St Helena from a little child at play?'
What makes you want to wander there with all the world between?
Oh, Mother, call your son again or else he'll run away.
(*No one thinks of winter when the grass is green!*)

'How far is St Helena from a fight in Paris street?'
I haven't time to answer now – the men are falling fast.
The guns begin to thunder, and the drums begin to beat.
(*If you take the first step, you will take the last!*)

'How far is St Helena from the field of Austerlitz?'
You couldn't hear me if I told – so loud the cannons roar.
But not so far for people who are living by their wits.
(*'Gay go up' means 'Gay go down' the wide world o'er!*)

'How far is St Helena from an Emperor of France?'
I cannot see – I cannot tell – the Crowns they dazzle so.
The Kings sit down to dinner, and the Queens stand up to dance.
(After open weather you may look for snow!)

'How far is St Helena from the Capes of Trafalgar?'
A longish way – a longish way – with ten year more to run.
It's South across the water underneath a falling star.
(What you cannot finish you must leave undone!)

'How far is St Helena from the Beresina ice?'
An ill way – a chill way – the ice begins to crack.

Napoleon's funeral procession, St Helena, 1821

But not so far for gentlemen who never took advice.
(When you can't go forward you must e'en come back!)

'How far is St Helena from the field of Waterloo?'
A near way – a clear way – the ship will take you soon.
A pleasant place for gentlemen with little left to do.
(Morning never tries you till the afternoon!)

'How far from St Helena to the Gate of Heaven's Grace?'
That no one knows – that no one knows – and no one ever will.
But fold your hands across your heart and cover up your face,
And after all your trapesings, child, lie still!

4 TOMMY ATKINS AND THE YEARS BEFORE ARMAGEDDON

For our first three programmes we had some of the poems and verses and ballads and jingles that Rudyard Kipling wrote about English history from the mists of antiquity until the death of Napoleon in 1821. After 1821 Kipling becomes rather a chronicler than a popular historian. As historian, the middle of the nineteenth century doesn't seem to have struck a responsive note in him, and he's given us nothing on the Industrial Revolution, nothing, rather surprisingly, on the birth of the railways (though he wrote some grand stuff on later, mostly American, railways). He didn't write about the Reform Bills – perhaps we wouldn't expect him to – and he wrote nothing on the Crimean War or the American Civil War. But from the 1880s he was deeply moved by the events of his own time, and his often passionate chronicling is now history to us.

No one in the late nineteenth century meant more to Kipling than Tommy Atkins, the common British soldier. It was to Tommy Atkins that he dedicated his famous books of poems, *Barrack-Room Ballads,* with a poem ending – 'And, Thomas, here's my best respects to you', and it is to Tommy Atkins that the first part of this programme is given.

We start with a poem which is said, but not on very good evidence, to have outraged Queen Victoria:

THE WIDOW AT WINDSOR   [*Voice: Cockney*]

'Ave you 'eard o' the Widow at Windsor
  With a hairy gold crown on 'er 'ead?
She 'as ships on the foam – she 'as millions at 'ome,
  An' she pays us poor beggars in red.
    (Ow, poor beggars in red!)
There's 'er nick on the cavalry 'orses,
  There's 'er mark on the medical stores –
An' 'er troopers you'll find with a fair wind be'ind
  That takes us to various wars.
    (Poor beggars! – barbarious wars!)

Then 'ere's to the Widow at Windsor,
    An' 'ere's to the stores an' the guns,
The men an' the 'orses what makes up the forces
    O' Missis Victorier's sons.
    (Poor beggars! Victorier's sons!)

Walk wide o' the Widow at Windsor,
    For 'alf o' Creation she owns:
We 'ave bought 'er the same with the sword an' the flame,
    An' we've salted it down with our bones.
      (Poor beggars! – it's blue with our bones!)
Hands off o' the sons o' the Widow,
    Hands off o' the goods in 'er shop.
For the Kings must come down an' the Emperors frown
    When the Widow at Windsor says 'Stop!'
      (Poor beggars! – we're sent to say 'Stop!')
        Then 'ere's to the Lodge o' the Widow,
          From the Pole to the Tropics it runs –
        To the Lodge that we tile with the rank an' the file,
          An' open in form with the guns.
      (Poor beggars! – it's always they guns!)

We 'ave 'eard o' the Widow at Windsor,
    It's safest to leave 'er alone:
For 'er sentries we stand by the sea an' the land
    Wherever the bugles are blown.
      (Poor beggars! – an' don't we get blown!)
Take 'old o' the Wings o' the Mornin',
    An' flop round the earth till you're dead;
But you won't get away from the tune that they play
    To the bloomin' old rag over'ead.
      (Poor beggars! – it's 'ot over'ead!)
        Then 'ere's to the Sons o' the Widow,
          Wherever, 'owever they roam.
        'Ere's all they desire, an' if they require
          A speedy return to their 'ome.
      (Poor beggars! – they'll never see 'ome!)

In the next poem, about a soldier who doesn't see home again, Kipling uses a traditional ballad form, and so gives a contemporary immediacy to a situation as old as armies:

SOLDIER, SOLDIER   [*Voices: Suburban London*]

'Soldier, soldier come from the wars,
'Why don't you march with my true love?'
'We're fresh from off the ship an' 'e's, maybe, give the slip,
'An' you'd best go look for a new love.'

New love! True love!
Best go look for a new love,
The dead they cannot rise, an' you'd better dry your eyes,
An' you'd best go look for a new love.

'Soldier, soldier come from the wars,
'What did you see o' my true love?'
'I seen 'im serve the Queen in a suit o' rifle-green,
'An' you'd best go look for a new love.'

'Soldier, soldier come from the wars,
'Did ye see no more o' my true love?'
'I seen 'im runnin' by when the shots begun to fly –
'But you'd best go look for a new love.'

'Soldier, soldier come from the wars,
'Did aught take 'arm to my true love?'
'I couldn't see the fight, for the smoke it lay so white –
'And you'd best go look for a new love.'

'Soldier, soldier come from the wars,
'I'll up an' tend to my true love!'
' 'E's lying on the dead with a bullet through 'is 'ead,
'An' you'd best go look for a new love.'

'Soldier, soldier come from the wars,
'I'll down an' die with my true love!'
'The pit we dug'll 'ide 'im an' the twenty more beside 'im –
'An' you'd best go look for a new love.'

'Soldier, soldier come from the wars,
'Do you bring no sign from my true love?'
'I bring a lock of 'air that 'e allus used to wear,
'An' you'd best go look for a new love.'

'Soldier, soldier come from the wars,
'O then I know it's true I've lost my true love!'
'An' I tell you truth again – when you've lost the feel o' pain
'You'd best take me for your new love.'

 True love! New love!
 Best take 'im for a new love,
 The dead they cannot rise, an' you'd better dry your eyes
 An' you'd best take 'im for your new love.

Of course, Tommy Atkins wasn't only a Cockney, as people will know who remember Kipling's *Soldiers Three*, the Cockney, the Yorkshireman and the Irishman. It is the voice of the last that we chose for Kipling's perhaps best-known poem 'Danny Deever':

DANNY DEEVER [*Voice: Southern Irish*]

'What are the bugles blowin' for?' said Files-on-Parade.
'To turn you out, to turn you out,' the Colour-Sergeant said.
'What makes you look so white, so white?' said Files-on-Parade.
'I'm dreadin' what I've got to watch,' the Colour-Sergeant said.
 For they're hangin' Danny Deever, you can hear the Dead March play,
 The Regiment's in 'ollow square – they're hangin' him to-day;
 They've taken of his buttons off an' cut his stripes away,
 An' they're hangin' Danny Deever in the mornin'.

'What makes the rear-rank breathe so 'ard?' said Files-on-Parade.
'It's bitter cold, it's bitter cold,' the Colour-Sergeant said.
'What makes that front-rank man fall down?' said Files-on-Parade.
'A touch o' sun, a touch o' sun,' the Colour-Sergeant said.
 They are hangin' Danny Deever, they are marchin' of 'im round,
 They 'ave 'alted Danny Deever by 'is coffin on the ground;

[78]

An' 'e'll swing in 'arf a minute for a sneakin' shootin' hound –
O they're hangin' Danny Deever in the mornin'!

' 'Is cot was right-'and cot to mine,' said Files-on-Parade.
' 'E's sleepin' out an' far to-night,' the Colour-Sergeant said.
' I've drunk 'is beer a score o' times,' said Files-on-Parade.
' 'E's drinkin' bitter beer alone,' the Colour-Sergeant said.
   They are hangin' Danny Deever, you must mark 'im to 'is place,
   For 'e shot a comrade sleepin' – you must look 'im in the face;
   Nine 'undred of 'is county an' the Regiment's disgrace,
   While they're hangin' Danny Deever in the mornin'.

'What's that so black agin the sun?' said Files-on-Parade.
'It's Danny fightin' 'ard for life,' the Colour-Sergeant said.
'What's that that whimpers over'ead?' said Files-on-Parade.
'It's Danny's soul that's passin' now,' the Colour-Sergeant said.
   For they're done with Danny Deever, you can 'ear the quickstep play,
   The Regiment's in column, an' they're marchin' us away;
   Ho! the young recruits are shakin', an' they'll want their beer to-day,
   After hangin' Danny Deever in the mornin'!

Poems about soldiers must often be poems about death. Here's another poem about a dead soldier:

'FOLLOW ME 'OME'   [*Voice: Southern Irish*]

   There was no one like 'im, 'Orse or Foot,
   Nor any o' the Guns I knew;
   An' because it was so, why, o' course 'e went an' died,
   Which is just what the best men do.

   So it's knock out your pipes an' follow me!
   An' it's finish up your swipes an' follow me!
   Oh, 'ark to the big drum callin',
   Follow me – follow me 'ome!

'Is mare she neighs the 'ole day long,
She paws the 'ole night through,
An' she won't take 'er feed 'cause o' waitin' for 'is step,
Which is just what a beast would do.

'Is girl she goes with a bombardier
Before 'er month is through;
An' the banns are up in church, for she's got the beggar
  hooked,
Which is just what a girl would do.

We fought 'bout a dog – last week it were –
No more than a round or two;
But I strook 'im cruel 'ard, an' I wish I 'adn't now,
Which is just what a man can't do.

'E was all that I 'ad in the way of a friend,
An' I've 'ad to find one new;
But I'd give my pay an' stripe for to get the beggar back,
Which it's just too late to do!

So it's knock out your pipes an' follow me!
An' it's finish up your swipes an' follow me!
Oh, 'ark to the fifes a-crawlin'!
Follow me – follow me 'ome!

Take 'im away! 'E's gone where the best men go.
Take 'im away! An' the gun-wheels turnin' slow.
Take 'im away! There's more from the place 'e come.
Take 'im away, with the limber an' the drum.

For it's 'Three rounds blank' an' follow me,
An' it's 'Thirteen rank' an' follow me;
Oh, passin' the love o' women,
Follow me – follow me 'ome!

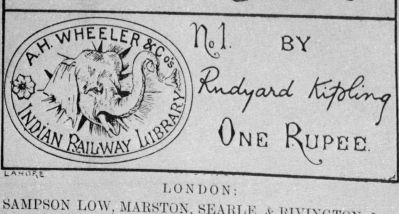

LONDON:
SAMPSON LOW, MARSTON, SEARLE, & RIVINGTON, Ld.,
ST. DUNSTAN'S HOUSE, FETTER LANE, E.C.
NEW YORK: BROMFIELD & CO., 658 BROADWAY.

Cover from a paperback edition of Kipling's 'Soldiers Three'

Kipling's poems about soldiers aren't only poems about death. They're also about the ordinary everyday life of soldiers whom the general public still despised as brutal and licentious. Kipling never accepted this, but he wasn't mealy-mouthed about the coarse realities of soldiers' lives. As he put it once, 'single men in barricks don't grow into plaster saints'. The next poem is about a soldier who was a long way from being any kind of a saint:

THE SERGEANT'S WEDDIN'　　[*Voice: Cockney*]

'E was warned agin 'er –
　　That's what made 'im look;
She was warned agin' 'im
　　That is why she took.
'Wouldn't 'ear no reason,
　　'Went an' done it blind;
We know all about 'em,
　　They've got all to find!

Cheer for the Sergeant's weddin' –
　　Give 'em one cheer more!
Grey gun-'orses in the lando,
　　An' a rogue is married to an 'ore.

What's the use o' tellin'
　　'Arf the lot she's been?
'E's a bloomin' robber,
　　An' 'e keeps canteen.
'Ow did 'e get 'is buggy?
　　Gawd, you needn't ask!
'Made 'is forty gallon
　　Out of every cask!

Watch 'im, with 'is 'air cut,
　　Count us filin' by –
Won't the Colonel praise 'is
　　Pop - u - lar - i - ty!
We 'ave scores to settle –
　　Scores for more than beer;

[82]

She's the girl to pay 'em –
    That is why we're 'ere!

See the Chaplain thinkin'?
    See the women smile?
Twig the married winkin'
    As they take the aisle?
Keep your side-arms quiet,
    Dressin' by the Band.
Ho! You 'oly beggars,
    Cough be'ind your 'and!

Now it's done an' over,
    'Ear the organ squeak,
' *'Voice that breathed o'er Eden'* –
    Ain't she got the cheek!
White an' laylock ribbons,
    'Think yourself so fine!
I'd pray Gawd to take yer
    'Fore I made yer mine!

Escort to the kerridge,
    Wish 'im luck, the brute!
Chuck the slippers after –
    (Pity 'tain't a boot!)
Bowin' like a lady,
    Blushin' like a lad –
'Oo would say to see 'em
    Both is rotten bad?

Cheer for the Sergeant's weddin' –
    Give 'em one cheer more!
Grey gun-'orses in the lando,
    An' a rogue is married to an 'ore.

Although Kipling wrote so many poems in admiration of common men, he's always had a reputation for admiring the upper classes. But he didn't, as such: 'the flannelled fools at the wicket', he once called them. The upper classes, like the lower, have to deserve his admiration to make the grade, and, in fact, many of his upper-class poems are of pity for the gentlemen who *didn't* make the grade – the cowards, the ne'er-do-wells, the failures, the black sheep – as in this next poem about a not uncommon figure in the Victorian army, the gentleman ranker:

GENTLEMEN-RANKERS   [*Voice: La-di-dah Gentry*]

To the legion of the lost ones, to the cohort of the damned,
To my brethren in their sorrow overseas,
Sings a gentleman of England cleanly bred, machinely crammed,
And a trooper of the Empress, if you please.
Yes, a trooper of the forces who has run his own six horses,
And faith he went the pace and went it blind,
And the world was more than kin while he held the ready tin,
But to-day the Sergeant's something less than kind.

     We're poor little lambs who've lost our way,
     Baa! Baa! Baa!
     We're little black sheep who've gone astray,
     Baa – aa – aa!
     Gentlemen-rankers out on the spree,
     Damned from here to Eternity,
     God ha' mercy on such as we,
     Baa! Yah! Bah!

Oh, it's sweet to sweat through stables, sweet to empty
   kitchen slops,
And it's sweet to hear the tales the troopers tell,
To dance with blowzy housemaids at the regimental hops
And thrash the cad who says you waltz too well.
Yes, it makes you cock-a-hoop to be 'Rider' to your troop,
And branded with a blasted worsted spur,
When you envy, O how keenly, one poor Tommy living cleanly
Who blacks your boots and sometimes calls you 'Sir'.

If the home we never write to, and the oaths we never keep,
And all we know most distant and most dear,
Across the snoring barrack-room return to break our sleep,

Can you blame us if we soak ourselves in beer?
When the drunken comrade mutters and the great guard-
    lantern gutters
And the horror of our fall is written plain,
Every secret, self-revealing on the aching whitewashed ceiling,
Do you wonder that we drug ourselves from pain?

We have done with Hope and Honour, we are lost to Love and
    Truth,
We are dropping down the ladder rung by rung,
And the measure of our torment is the measure of our youth.
God help us, for we knew the worst too young!
Our shame is clean repentance for the crime that brought the
    sentence,
  Our pride it is to know no spur of pride,
  And the Curse of Reuben holds us till an alien turf enfolds us
And we die, and none can tell Them where we died.
        We're poor little lambs who've lost our way,
        Baa! Baa! Baa!
        We're little black sheep who've gone astray,
        Baa – aa – aa!
        Gentlemen-rankers out on the spree,
        Damned from here to Eternity,
        God ha' mercy on such as we,
        Baa! Yah! Bah!

I once heard T. S. Eliot give a talk in which he said that the greatest influ-
ence on his own poetry was that of Rudyard Kipling, and since then I've
wondered if Eliot's lines about 'the damp souls of housemaids Sprouting
despondently at area gates' were an echo from Kipling's 'Mandalay',
another of Kipling's poems about a common soldier who served overseas and
lost his heart there:

MANDALAY   [*Voice: Cockney*]

By the old Moulmein Pagoda, lookin' lazy at the sea,
There's a Burma girl a-settin', and I know she thinks o' me;
For the wind is in the palm-trees, and the temple-bells they say:
'Come you back, you British soldier; come you back to Mandalay!'
    Come you back to Mandalay,
    Where the old Flotilla lay:
    Can't you 'ear their paddles chunkin' from Rangoon to Mandalay?
    On the road to Mandalay,
    Where the flyin'-fishes play,
    An' the dawn comes up like thunder outer China 'crost the Bay!

'Er petticoat was yaller an' 'er little cap was green,
An' 'er name was Supi-yaw-lat – jes' the same as Theebaw's Queen,
An' I seed her first a-smokin' of a whackin' white cheroot,
An' a-wastin' Christian kisses on an' 'eathen idol's foot:
    Bloomin' idol made o' mud –
    Wot they called the Great Gawd Budd –
    Plucky lot she cared for idols when I kissed 'er where she stud!
    On the road to Mandalay,
    Where the flyin'-fishes play,
    An' the dawn comes up like thunder outer China 'crost the Bay!

When the mist was on the rice-fields an' the sun was droppin' slow,
She'd git 'er little banjo an' she'd sing '*Kulla-lo-lo!*'
With 'er arm upon my shoulder an' 'er cheek agin my cheek
We useter watch the steamers an' the *hathis* pilin' teak.
    Elephints a-pilin' teak
    In the sludgy, squdgy creek,
    Where the silence 'ung that 'eavy you was 'arf afraid to speak!
    On the road to Mandalay,
    Where the flyin'-fishes play,
    An' the dawn comes up like thunder outer China 'crost the Bay!

But that's all shove be'ind me – long ago an' fur away,
An' there ain't no buses runnin' from the Bank to Mandalay;
An' I'm learnin' 'ere in London what the ten-year soldier tells:

'If you've 'eard the East a-callin', you won't never 'eed naught else.'
    No! you won't 'eed nothin' else
    But them spicy garlic smells,
    An' the sunshine an' the palm-trees an' the tinkly temple-bells;
    On the road to Mandalay,
    Where the flyin'-fishes play,
    An' the dawn comes up like thunder outer China 'crost the Bay!

I am sick o' wastin' leather on these gritty pavin'-stones,
An' the blasted English drizzle wakes the fever in my bones;
'Tho' I walks with fifty 'ousemaids outer Chelsea to the Strand,
An' they talks a lot o' lovin', but wot do they understand?
    Beefy face an' grubby 'and –
    Law! wot do they understand?
    I've a neater, sweeter maiden in a cleaner, greener land!
    On the road to Mandalay,
    Where the flyin-fishes play,
    An' the dawn comes up like thunder outer China 'crost the Bay!

Ship me somewheres east of Suez, where the best is like the worst,
Where there aren't no Ten Commandments an' a man can raise a
    thirst;
For the temple-bells are callin', an' it's there that I would be –
By the old Moulmein Pagoda, looking lazy at the sea;
    On the road to Mandalay,
    Where the old Flotilla lay,
    With our sick beneath the awnings when we went to Mandalay!
    O the road to Mandalay,
    Where the flyin'-fishes play,
    An' the dawn comes up like thunder outer China 'crost the Bay!

We could stay in the Empire – but Kipling's British Empire is another long story and now we are concerned with England: England, where things were going wrong. We're in the 1890s now. There had been the great dockers' strike of 1889. The growing power and activity of the Trades Unions seemed ominous to many, and the Fabian socialists were talking their heads off.

Much literature and art had deliberately turned to decadence: the *Yellow Book* first appeared in 1894, Oscar Wilde's trial was in 1895. The Liberal Party under Gladstone had supported, in Ireland, people whom Kipling saw as no better than murderers. Even the British Army had failed, in the Sudan, and Gordon had died at Khartoum. In 1891 the newspapers reported an incident that seemed to Kipling hideously significant: an English flag fell from a burning building into the flames and a watching crowd cheered at the sight:

THE ENGLISH FLAG   [*Voice: Gentry*]

Winds of the World, give answer! They are whimpering to and fro –
And what should they know of England who only England know? –
The poor little street-bred people that vapour and fume and brag,
They are lifting their heads in the stillness to yelp at the English Flag!

In 1899 came the Boer War, fought not only by the British Army but also by British volunteers, a war against the Dutch South Africans under Paul Kruger. Many Englishmen saw this war as unjustified imperial oppression: Little Englanders, these were called. But to Kipling the Boer War seemed a great opportunity, not only for training soldiers for a greater war he could already see distantly looming, but also a chance of redemption for the poor little street-bred people. To raise money for the troops Kipling wrote some verses which, he said, had some elements of direct appeal but lacked poetry. Printed as leaflets and on handkerchiefs and scarves, sung to a tune by Sir Arthur Sullivan, recited at popular concerts or ground out on barrel-organs, they raised a fund of a quarter of a million pounds:

THE ABSENT-MINDED BEGGAR   [*Voice: Cockney*]

When you've shouted 'Rule Britannia', when you've sung 'God
   save the Queen',
When you've finished killing Kruger with your mouth,
Will you kindly drop a shilling in my little tambourine
For a gentleman in khaki ordered South?
He's an absent-minded beggar, and his weaknesses are great –

R. Caton Woodville
1899

"A gentleman in kharki."

But we and Paul must take him as we find him –
He is out on active service, wiping something off a slate –
And he's left a lot of little things behind him!
Duke's son – cook's son – son of a hundred kings –
(Fifty thousand horse and foot going to Table Bay!)
Each of 'em doing his country's work
    (and who's to look after their things?)
Pass the hat for your credit's sake,
    and pay – pay – pay!

There are girls he married secret, asking no permission to,
For he knew he wouldn't get it if he did.
There is gas and coals and vittles, and the house-rent falling due,
And it's more than rather likely there's a kid.
There are girls he walked with casual. They'll be sorry now he's
    gone,
For an absent-minded beggar they will find him,
But it ain't the time for sermons with the winter coming on.
We must help the girl that Tommy's left behind him!
Cook's son – Duke's son – son of a belted Earl –
Son of a Lambeth publican – it's all the same today!
Each of 'em doing his country's work
    (and who's to look after the girl?)
Pass the hat for your credit's sake,
    and pay – pay – pay!

There are families by thousands, far too proud to beg or speak,
And they'll put their sticks and bedding up the spout,
And they'll live on half o' nothing, paid 'em punctual once a week,
'Cause the man that earns the wage is ordered out.
He's an absent-minded beggar, but he heard his country call,
And his reg'ment didn't need to send to find him!
He chucked his job and joined it – so the job before us all
Is to help the home that Tommy's left behind him!
Duke's job – cook's job – gardener, baronet, groom,
Mews or palace or paper-shop, there's someone gone away!
Each of 'em doing his country's work

(and who's to look after the room?)
Pass the hat for your credit's sake,
   and pay – pay – pay!

Let us manage so as, later, we can look him in the face,
And tell him – what he'd very much prefer –
That, while he saved the Empire, his employer saved his place,
And his mates (that's you and me) looked out for *her*.
He's an absent-minded beggar and he may forget it all,
But we do not want his kiddies to remind him
That we sent 'em to the workhouse while their daddy hammered Paul,
So we'll help the homes that Tommy left behind him!
Cook's home – Duke's home – home of a millionaire,
(Fifty thousand horse and foot going to Table Bay!)
Each of 'em doing his country's work
   (and what have you got to spare?)
Pass the hat for your credit's sake,
   and pay – pay – pay!

For the volunteers who had seen a new kind of life in the wide open spaces of the South African veldt, homecoming wouldn't always be easy. And once again Kipling wrote of the soldier, this time the volunteer soldier, who saw a richer life away from England; and this time there is a deepening of the sour note about home already sounding in 'Mandalay':

CHANT-PAGAN   [*Voice: Sussex*]

Me that 'ave been what I've been –
Me that 'ave gone where I've gone –
Me that 'ave seen what I've seen –
  'Ow can I ever take on
With awful old England again,
An' 'ouses both sides of the street,
And 'edges two sides of the lane,
And the parson an' gentry between,
An' touchin' my 'at when we meet –
Me that 'ave been what I've been?

[91]

Me that 'ave watched 'arf a world
'Eave up all shiny with dew,
Kopje on kop to the sun,
An' as soon as the mist let 'em through
Our 'elios winkin' like fun –
Three sides of a ninety-mile square,
Over valleys as big as a shire –
'Are ye there? Are ye there? Are ye there?'
An' then the blind drum of our fire . . .
An' I'm rollin' 'is lawns for the Squire,

Me!

Me that 'ave rode through the dark
Forty mile, often, on end,
Along the Ma'ollisberg Range,
With only the stars for my mark
An' only the night for my friend,
An' things runnin' off as you pass,
An' things jumpin' up in the grass,
An' the silence, the shine an' the size
Of the 'igh, unexpressible skies –
I am takin' some letters almost
As much as a mile to the post,
An' 'mind you come back with the change!'

Me!

Me that saw Barberton took
When we dropped through the clouds on their 'ead,
An' they 'ove the guns over and fled –
Me that was through Di'mond 'Ill,
An' Pieters an' Springs an' Belfast –
From Dundee to Vereeniging all –
Me that stuck out to the last
(An' five bloomin' bars on my chest) –
I am doin' my Sunday-school best,
By the 'elp of the Squire an' 'is wife
(Not to mention the 'ousemaid an' cook),
To come in an' 'ands up an' be still,
An' honestly work for my bread,

My livin' in that state of life
To which it shall please God to call
Me!

Me that 'ave followed my trade
In the place where the Lightnin's are made;
'Twixt the Rains and the Sun and the Moon –
Me that lay down an' got up
Three years with the sky for my roof –
That 'ave ridden my 'unger an' thirst
Six thousand raw mile on the hoof,
With the Vaal and the Orange for cup,
An' the Brandwater Basin for dish, –
Oh! it's 'ard to be'ave as they wish
(Too 'ard, an' a little too soon),
I'll 'ave to think over it first –
Me!

I will arise an' get 'ence –
I will trek South and make sure
If it's only my fancy or not
That the sunshine of England is pale,
And the breezes of England are stale,
An' there's somethin' gone small with the lot.
For *I* know of a sun an' a wind,
An' some plains and a mountain be'ind,
An' some graves by a barb-wire fence,
An' a Dutchman I've fought 'oo might give
Me a job were I ever inclined
To look in an' offsaddle an' live
Where there's neither a road nor a tree –
But only my Maker an' me,
And I think it will kill me or cure,
So I think I will go there an' see.
Me!

While some of the English were enjoying that golden summer of peace and prosperity that seems to have lasted, for the fortunate ones, from 1901 till August 1914, others, and Kipling among them, were worried stiff. Something was rotten, something was wrong; perhaps with England herself whose skills and responsibilities seemed to have been forgotten. Kipling's best poem about the anxieties of these inter-war years, as they proved to be, has a more universal application than the rather topical piece we've just heard:

THE DYKES   [*Voice: East Anglian*]

We have no heart for the fishing – we have no hand for the oar –
All that our fathers taught us of old pleases us now no more.
All that our own hearts bid us believe we doubt where we do not deny –
There is no proof in the bread we eat nor rest in the toil we ply.

Look you, our foreshore stretches far through sea-gate, dyke, and groin –
Made land all, that our fathers made, where the flats and the fairway join.
They forced the sea a sea-league back. They died, and their work stood
    fast.
We were born to peace in the lee of the dykes, but the time of our peace is
    past.

Far off, the full tide clambers and slips, mouthing and testing all,
Nipping the flanks of the water-gates, baying along the wall;
Turning the shingle, returning the shingle, changing the set of the sand . . .
We are too far from the beach, men say, to know how the outworks stand.

So we come down, uneasy, to look; uneasily pacing the beach.
These are the dykes our fathers made: we have never known a breach.
Time and again has the gale blown by and we were not afraid;
Now we come only to look at the dykes – at the dykes our fathers made.

O'er the marsh where the homesteads cower apart the harried sunlight
    flies,
Shifts and considers, wanes and recovers, scatters and sickens and dies –
An evil ember bedded in ash – a spark blown west by the wind . . .
We are surrendered to night and the sea – the gale and the tide behind!

At the bridge of the lower saltings the cattle gather and blare,
Roused by the feet of running men, dazed by the lantern-glare.
Unbar and let them away for their lives – the levels drown as they stand,
Where the flood-wash forces the sluices aback and the ditches deliver
  inland.

Ninefold deep to the top of the dykes the galloping breakers stride,
And their overcarried spray is a sea – a sea on the landward side.
Coming, like stallions they paw with their hooves, going they snatch with
  their teeth,
Till the bents and the furze and the sand are dragged out, and the old-time
  hurdles beneath.

Bid men gather fuel for fire, the tar, the oil, and the tow –
Flame we shall need, not smoke, in the dark if the riddled sea-banks go.
Bid the ringers watch in the tower (who knows how the dawn shall prove?)
Each with his rope between his feet and the trembling bells above.

Now we can only wait till the day, wait and apportion our shame.
These are the dykes our fathers left, but we would not look to the same.
Time and again were we warned of the dykes, time and again we delayed:
Now, it may fall, we have slain our sons, as our fathers we have betrayed.

      .   .   .   .

Walking along the wreck of the dykes, watching the work of the seas!
These were the dykes our fathers made to our great profit and ease.
But the peace is gone and the profit is gone, with the old sure days
  withdrawn . . .
That our own houses show as strange when we come back in the dawn!

5 THE GREAT WAR AND AFTER

On August the fourth, 1914, we went to war. To Rudyard Kipling this war was the Armageddon that he, and a few, too few other people had been expecting at least since the beginning of the century. And Armageddon it proved to be. For the nation, it was a war that lost us almost a generation of young men, and for the men who fought, it was probably the most horrible war in British history.

Today, when we think of the poets of that war, the names that first come to mind would be Rupert Brooke, Wilfred Owen, Julian Grenfell, Siegfried Sassoon: young men, and out of the four I've named, three of them died in it. Few people would think of Rudyard Kipling among the war poets, but he *was* a war poet, and often a painfully compelling one.

When the war began, in 1914, Kipling was too old to fight, except with his pen, and we shouldn't expect from him the compassionate comradeship with the enemy soldiers of, say, Wilfred Owen. Kipling had never liked the Germans. He came to hate them and his first war poem, which was published in *The Times* on the second of September 1914, expressed the nation's mood, too, as it went into the war:

'FOR ALL WE HAVE AND ARE'   [*Voice: Gentry*]

> For all we have and are,
> For all our children's fate,
> Stand up and take the war.
> The Hun is at the gate!
> Our world has passed away,
> In wantonness o'erthrown.
> There is nothing left to-day
> But steel and fire and stone!
>   Though all we knew depart,
>   The old Commandments stand:—
>   'In courage keep your heart,
>   In strength lift up your hand.'

Once more we hear the word
That sickened earth of old:—
'No law except the Sword
Unsheathed and uncontrolled.'
Once more it knits mankind,
Once more the nations go
To meet and break and bind
A crazed and driven foe.

Comfort, content, delight,
The ages' slow-bought gain,
They shrivelled in a night.
Only ourselves remain
To face the naked days
In silent fortitude,
Through perils and dismays
Renewed and re-renewed.
　　Though all we made depart,
　　The old Commandments stand:—
　　'In patience keep your heart,
　　In strength lift up your hand.'

No easy hope or lies
Shall bring us to our goal,
But iron sacrifice
Of body, will, and soul.
There is but one task for all –
One life for each to give.
What stands if Freedom fall?
Who dies if England live?

The war at sea was as vital and as wasteful in the Great War as it was in
Hitler's War a generation later. One of Kipling's most moving poems about
it used that question-and-answer ballad form by which he so often set an
immediate tragedy in a larger historical context:

'Have you news of my boy Jack?'
  Not this tide.
'When d'you think that he'll come back?'
  Not with this wind blowing, and this tide.

'Has any one else had word of him?'
  Not this tide.
For what is sunk will hardly swim,
  Not with this wind blowing, and this tide.

'Oh, dear, what comfort can I find?'
  None this tide,
  Nor any tide,
Except he did not shame his kind –
  Not even with that wind blowing, and that tide.

Then hold your head up all the more,
  This tide,
  And every tide;
Because he was the son you bore,
  And gave to that wind blowing and that tide!

But in most of Kipling's war poems he left the traditional verse forms for more direct, more immediate expression, and on the war at sea his outstanding poem is the simple 'Mine Sweepers':

MINE SWEEPERS   [*Voice: Southern English*]

Dawn off the Foreland – the young flood making
  Jumbled and short and steep –
Black in the hollows and bright where it's breaking –
  Awkward water to sweep.
  'Mines reported in the fairway,
  'Warn all traffic and detain.
' 'Sent up *Unity, Claribel, Assyrian, Stormcock,* and *Golden Gain.*'

Noon off the Foreland – the first ebb making
    Lumpy and strong in the bight.
Boom after boom, and the golf-hut shaking
    And the jackdaws wild with fright!
    'Mines located in the fairway,
    'Boats now working up the chain,
'Sweepers – *Unity, Claribel, Assyrian, Stormcock,* and *Golden Gain.*'

Dusk off the Foreland – the last light going
    And the traffic crowding through,
And five damned trawlers with their syreens blowing
    Heading the whole review!
    'Sweep completed in the fairway.
    'No more mines remain.
' 'Sent back *Unity, Claribel, Assyrian, Stormcock,* and *Golden Gain.*'

Not all Kipling's war poems are so simple or so easily understood. This poem on the fighting in France is one of the strangest:

GETHSEMANE   [*Voice: Suburban London*]

The Garden called Gethsemane
    In Picardy it was,
And there the people came to see
    The English soldiers pass.
We used to pass – we used to pass
    Or halt, as might be,
And ship our masks in case of gas
    Beyond Gethsemane.

The Garden called Gethsemane,
    It held a pretty lass,
But all the time she talked to me
    I prayed my cup might pass.
The officer sat on the chair,
    The men lay on the grass,

And all the time we halted there
    I prayed my cup might pass.

It didn't pass – it didn't pass –
    It didn't pass from me.
I drank it when we met the gas
    Beyond Gethsemane!

One thing Kipling had in common with the younger war poets was a bitter hatred for the bungling politicians, as he saw them, who, through ignorance or carelessness or ambition, sacrificed the soldiers. Such an episode was the Mesopotamian campaign of late 1915, when the Indian Government, at the instance of the British Cabinet, sent a brigade under General Townsend to drive the Turks out of Basra on the Persian Gulf. This Townsend successfully achieved. Unfortunately, and for no adequate reason, the British force went on inland towards Baghdad. They were trapped and besieged in the filthy mud heap of Kut-el-Amara on the Tigris River, and after a five-month siege the British forces surrendered unconditionally to the Turks.

    General Townsend went into comfortable internment, the officers into endurable prison camps. The men – I quote the war historian Cruttwell – 'The men were herded like animals across the desert, flogged, kicked, raped, tortured and murdered. More than two-thirds of the British rank and file were dead before the war ended'. On this beastly episode Kipling wrote his poem 'Mesopotamia':

MESOPOTAMIA   *[Voice: Gentry]*

They shall not return to us, the resolute, the young,
    The eager and whole-hearted whom we gave:
But the men who left them thriftily to die in their own dung,
    Shall they come with years and honour to the grave?

They shall not return to us, the strong men coldly slain
    In sight of help denied from day to day:
But the men who edged their agonies and chid them in their pain,
    Are they too strong and wise to put away?

Our dead shall not return to us while Day and Night divide –
    Never while the bars of sunset hold.
But the idle-minded overlings who quibbled while they died,
    Shall they thrust for high employments as of old?

Shall we only threaten and be angry for an hour?
    When the storm is ended shall we find
How softly but how swiftly they have sidled back to power
    By the favour and contrivance of their kind?

Even while they soothe us, while they promise large amends,
    Even while they make a show of fear,
Do they call upon their debtors, and take counsel with their friends,
    To confirm and re-establish each career?

Their lives cannot repay us – their death could not undo –
    The shame that they have laid upon our race.
But the slothfulness that wasted and the arrogance that slew,
    Shall we leave it unabated in its place?

This same bitterness colours many of the epitaphs Kipling wrote for the war dead. Here are a few of them. First, for a dead statesman:

(EPITAPHS OF THE WAR: 1914–18)

[*Voice: Welsh-English*]

I could not dig: I dared not rob:
Therefore I lied to please the mob.
Now all my lies are proved untrue
And I must face the men I slew.
What tale shall serve me here among
Mine angry and defrauded young?

The next epitaph is called 'Common Form':

[*Voice: Gentry*]

If any question why we died,
Tell them, because our fathers lied.

Now an epitaph for a battery of guns that ran out of ammunition:

[*Voice: North-Country English*]

If any mourn us in the workshop, say
We died because the shift kept holiday.

Epitaph for a coward:

[*Voice: Gentry*]

I could not look on Death, which being known,
Men led me to him, blindfold and alone.

The calmest of these epitaphs is written in an older form. It is called 'The Bridegroom':

[*Voice: Gentry*]

Call me not false, beloved,
    If, from thy scarce-known breast
So little time removed,
    In other arms I rest.

For this more ancient bride,
    Whom coldly I embrace,
Was constant at my side
    Before I saw thy face.

Our marriage, often set –
    By miracle delayed
At last is consummate,
    And cannot be unmade.

Live, then, whom Life shall cure,
    Almost, of Memory,
And leave us to endure
    Its immortality.

FOR KING AND COUNTRY: OFFICERS ON THE ROLL OF HONOUR.

PHOTOGRAPHS BY CENTRAL PRESS, MAYTYPE, ELLIOTT AND FRY, BASSANO, ILLUSTRATIONS BURRAL, STUART, LANGFIER, WYKEHAM, CASWALL SMITH, BACON, ANNAN, CONREL,

LIEUT. WILFRED GRAHAM SALMON,
Royal Flying Corps. Killed while aiding in the defence of London in a recent enemy air-raid.

MAJOR (ACTING LIEUT.-COL.) R. J. F. INGHAM, D.S.O.,
R.G.A. Second son of Judge Ingham, of Sugwas Court, Hereford.

MAJOR H. D. HARVEY-KELLY, D.S.O.,
R. Irish Regt. (attd. R.F.C.). Son of late Col. H. H. Harvey-Kelly, I.A., and of Mrs. Harvey-Kelly, Buckingham.

LIEUT. T. FARQUHAR LUCAS.
R. Warwickshire Regt. and R.F.C. Son of Sir Edward Lucas, Bt., North Gate, Regent's Park.

MAJOR LESLIE JACK COULTER, D.S.O.,
Australian Engineers. Awarded D.S.O., September 1916. Killed in action.

CAPT. THE REV. CECIL H. SCHOOLING,
Chaplain to the Forces. Son of Mr. and Mrs. Frederick Schooling, Bromley, Kent.

2ND LIEUT. JOHN E. R. YOUNG,
R.F.C. Fought a fleet of enemy aeroplanes, practically single-handed, in a recent London air-raid.

MAJOR PERCY R. M. COLLINS, D.S.O.,
R.G.A. Son of Mr. Henry M. Collins, late General Manager, in Australasia, of Reuter's.

LT. (TEMP. CAPT.) EVELYN MAXWELL WEBB,
K.R. Rifle Corps. Son of Mr. and Mrs. Walter Webb. Killed in action.

LIEUT.-COL. H. T. BELCHER, D.S.O.,
R.F.A. Son of the Rev. T. Hayes Belcher, Bramley Rectory, Basingstoke. Fought with distinction in S. Africa.

LIEUT.-COL. ALFRED J. SANSOM.
Royal Sussex Regiment. Has been officially reported as having been killed in action.

2ND LIEUT. W. T. BARRAT,
Manchester Regiment. Has been officially reported as having died of wounds.

MAJOR ANDREW J. RENDEL, M.C.,
R.F.A. Son of Mr. and Mrs. Rendel, Courtfield Road, S.W., and grandson of Sir Alexander Rendel.

CAPTAIN A. P. BREWIS,
Northumberland Fusiliers. Elder son of Mr. and Mrs. Alfred Brewis, Granville Road, Newcastle-on-Tyne. Killed in action.

LIEUT. ALEXANDER MANTLE.
London Regt. Son of Dr. Alfred Mantle, of Harrogate. Has been officially reported killed in action.

MAJOR W. MUIR HAYMAN, M.I.C.E., D.S.O.,
Royal Engineers. Son of Mr. Hayman, of Somerset Place, Glasgow.

2ND LIEUT. W. G. YATES,
Manchester Regt. Elder son of Mrs. Yates, of Lauriston Road, Preston Park, Brighton.

CAPT. RALPH DUNCAN ROBINSON,
Loyal North Lancs Regt. Son of Mr. William C. Robinson, of Melvin, High Park Avenue, Kew Gardens.

MAJOR BASIL ZIANI DE FERRANTI, M.C.,
R.G.A. Son of Dr. S. Z. de Ferranti, The Hall, Baslow, Derbyshire.

CAPT. MAURICE LAKE HILDER, M.C.,
Royal Fusiliers. Son of Mr. and Mrs. Edward Hilder, Wellington Road, Regent's Park.

America didn't enter The Great War until the second of April 1917. 'There's such a thing as being too proud to fight', President Wilson had said two years earlier. It was not an attitude that could appeal to the allies, and Kipling attacked it in a poem written in 1916, a poem that clearly shows how, fully to understand Kipling's verse, one must have some understanding of the language of the Bible and, indeed, of Christian theology:

THE QUESTION   [*Voice: New-England English*]

Brethren, how shall it fare with me
    When the war is laid aside,
If it be proven that I am he
    For whom a world has died?

If it be proven that all my good,
    And the greater good I will make,
Were purchased me by a multitude
    Who suffered for my sake?

That I was delivered by mere mankind
    Vowed to one sacrifice,
And not, as I hold them, battle-blind,
    But dying with open eyes?

That they did not ask me to draw the sword
    When they stood to endure their lot –
That they only looked to me for a word,
    And I answered I knew them not?

If it be found, when the battle clears,
    Their death has set me free,
Then how shall I live with myself through the years
    Which they have bought for me?

Brethren, how must it fare with me,
    Or how am I justified,
If it be proven that I am he
    For whom mankind has died –
If it be proven that I am he
    Who, being questioned, denied?

[106]

So far there has been no need to associate Kipling's life with his poems, except superficially. But for one of his most painful war poems, I think it would be right to recall that Kipling's only son, John, then aged eighteen, was reported wounded and missing after that 1915 massacre known as the Battle of Loos. His body was never found.

THE CHILDREN   [*Voice: Gentry*]

These were our children who died for our lands: they were dear in our
    sight.
  We have only the memory left of their home-treasured sayings and
    laughter.
  The price of our loss shall be paid to our hands, not another's hereafter.
Neither the Alien nor Priest shall decide on it. That is our right.
      But who shall return us the children?

At the hour the Barbarian chose to disclose his pretences,
  And raged against Man, they engaged, on the breasts that they bared
    for us,
  The first felon-stroke of the sword he had long-time prepared for us –
Their bodies were all our defence while we wrought our defences.

They bought us anew with their blood, forbearing to blame us,
Those hours which we had not made good when the Judgment o'ercame us.
They believed us and perished for it. Our statecraft, our learning
Delivered them bound to the Pit and alive to the burning
Whither they mirthfully hastened as jostling for honour –
Not since her birth has our Earth seen such worth loosed upon her.

Nor was their agony brief, or once only imposed on them.
  The wounded, the war-spent, the sick received no exemption:

[107]

Being cured they returned and endured and achieved our redemption,
Hopeless themselves of relief, till Death, marvelling, closed on them.

That flesh we had nursed from the first in all cleanness was given
To corruption unveiled and assailed by the malice of Heaven
By the heart-shaking jests of Decay where it lolled on the wires –
To be blanched or gay-painted by fumes – to be cindered by fires –
To be senselessly tossed and retossed in stale mutilation
From crater to crater. For this we shall take expiation.
    But who shall return us our children?

I have often had to tell you that I don't fully understand the poems I've
chosen. Now comes the one I understand least of all, a poem of the end of the
war called 'A Death-Bed'. It is certainly about the German Kaiser, the
All-Highest, as he was entitled. I think that in the first verse there is an
image of hanging: you remember the cry 'Hang the Kaiser'. The reference
to one who died in a prison yard was surely to Nurse Edith Cavell, the
English nurse shot by the Germans in Belgium for helping English prisoners
to escape. And I think that Kipling remembered that the Kaiser's father had
died of cancer of the throat. Whatever its full meaning, 'A Death-Bed' is a
horrible poem – but it's compelling:

A DEATH-BED   [*Voices: Gentry and German-accented English*]

'This is the State above the Law.
    The State exists for the State alone.'
*(This is a gland at the back of the jaw,
    And an answering lump by the collar-bone.)*

Some die shouting in gas or fire;
    Some die silent, by shell and shot.
Some die desperate, caught on the wire;
    Some die suddenly. This will not.

'Regis suprema voluntas Lex'
(It will follow the regular course of – throats.)
Some die pinned by the broken decks,
    Some die sobbing between the boats.

Some die eloquent, pressed to death
    By the sliding trench, as their friends can hear.
Some die wholly in half a breath.
    Some – give trouble for half a year.

'There is neither Evil nor Good in life
    Except as the needs of the State ordain.'
(Since it is rather too late for the knife,
    All we can do is to mask the pain.)

Some die saintly in faith and hope –
    One died thus in a prison-yard –
Some die broken by rape or the rope;
    Some die easily. This dies hard.

'I will dash to pieces who bar my way.
    Woe to the traitor! Woe to the weak!'
(Let him write what he wishes to say.
    It tires him out if he tries to speak.)

Some die quietly. Some abound
    In loud self-pity. Others spread
Bad morale through the cots around . . .
    This is a type that is better dead.

'The war was forced on me by my foes.
    All that I sought was the right to live.'
(Don't be afraid of a triple dose;
    The pain will neutralise half we give.

Here are the needles. See that he dies
    While the effects of the drug endure . . .
What is the question he asks with his eyes? –
    Yes, All-Highest, to God, be sure.)

The price of that war was terrible, for the living as well as the dead. Some of the living paid literally in money to be put in touch with their dead. Anyone who promised communications with the Other Side could find willing purchasers of the gift they claimed, and on this pathetic quest Kipling wrote his poem 'En-dor'. He prefaced it with a verse from the First Book of Samuel – 'Behold, there is a woman that hath a familiar spirit at En-dor' – the woman we call the Witch of En-dor.

EN-DOR   [*Voice: Suburban London*]

The road to En-dor is easy to tread
    For Mother or yearning Wife.
There, it is sure, we shall meet our Dead
    As they were even in life.
Earth has not dreamed of the blessing in store
For desolate hearts on the road to En-dor.

Whispers shall comfort us out of the dark –
    Hands – ah, God! – that we knew!
Visions and voices – look and hark! –
    Shall prove that the tale is true,
And that those who have passed to the further shore
May be hailed – at a price – on the road to En-dor.

But they are so deep in their new eclipse
    Nothing they say can reach,
Unless it be uttered by alien lips
    And framed in a stranger's speech.
The son must send word to the mother that bore,
Through an hireling's mouth. 'Tis the rule of En-dor.

And not for nothing these gifts are shown
    By such as delight our Dead.
They must twitch and stiffen and slaver and groan
    Ere the eyes are set in the head,
And the voice from the belly begins. Therefore,
We pay them a wage where they ply at En-dor.

Even so, we have need of faith
　　And patience to follow the clue.
Often, at first, what the dear one saith
　　Is babble, or jest, or untrue.
(Lying spirits perplex us sore
Till our loves – and their lives – are well known at En-dor) . . . .

Oh, the road to En-dor is the oldest road
　　And the craziest road of all!
Straight it runs to the Witch's abode,
　　As it did in the days of Saul,
And nothing has changed of the sorrow in store
　　For such as go down on the road to En-dor!

Another part of the price was paid by the many young men who came back
maimed: some maimed in their bodies, others in their minds:

THE MOTHER'S SON　　　[*Voice: Suburban-London*]

　　I have a dream – a dreadful dream –
　　　　A dream that is never done.
　　I watch a man go out of his mind,
　　　　And he is My Mother's Son.

　　They pushed him into a Mental Home,
　　　　And that is like the grave:
　　For they do not let you sleep upstairs,
　　　　And you aren't allowed to shave.

　　And it was *not* disease or crime
　　　　Which got him landed there,
　　But because They laid on My Mother's Son
　　　　More than a man could bear.

　　What with noise, and fear of death,
　　　　Waking, and wounds and cold,
　　They filled the Cup for My Mother's Son
　　　　Fuller than it could hold.

They broke his body and his mind
    And yet They made him live,
And They asked more of My Mother's Son
    Than any man could give.

For, just because he had not died,
    Nor been discharged nor sick.
They dragged it out with My Mother's Son
    Longer than he could stick. . . .

And no one knows when he'll get well –
    So, there he'll have to be:
And, 'spite of the beard in the looking-glass,
    I know that man is me!

Again, as in the 1900s, there wasn't much to hope for in the years that we now know, and Kipling feared, were the years between the wars. In 1932, a year before Hitler came to power in Germany, Kipling's unease crystalised into one of the last fine poems he wrote:

THE STORM CONE   [*Voice: Gentry*]

This is the midnight – let no star
Delude us – dawn is very far.
This is the tempest long foretold –
Slow to make head but sure to hold.

Stand by! The lull 'twixt blast and blast
Signals the storm is near, not past;
And worse than present jeopardy
May our forlorn to-morrow be.

If we have cleared the expectant reef,
Let no man look for his relief.
Only the darkness hides the shape
Of further peril to escape.

It is decreed that we abide
The weight of gale against the tide
And those huge waves the outer main
Sends in to set us back again.

They fall and whelm. We strain to hear
The pulses of her labouring gear,
Till the deep throb beneath us proves,
After each shudder and check, she moves!

She moves, with all save purpose lost,
To make her offing from the coast;
But, till she fetches open sea,
Let no man deem that he is free!

Four years after he wrote that prophetic poem, in 1936, Kipling died. I don't want to end with Kipling the chronicler but with Kipling the popular historian. In our first programme we started Kipling's English history in Kipling's Sussex, going backwards in time with Puck's song. Now we shall end in Kipling's Sussex with a poem that opens in Roman Britain where we began our story, a poem about what is most enduring in England's history, the land:

THE LAND   [*Voices: Gentry and Sussex*]

When Julius Fabricius, Sub-Prefect of the Weald,
In the days of Diocletian owned our Lower River-field,
He called to him Hobdenius – a Briton of the Clay,
Saying: 'What about that River-piece for layin' in to hay?'

And the aged Hobden answered: 'I remember as a lad
My father told your father that she wanted dreenin' bad.
An' the more that you neeglect her the less you'll get her clean.
Have it jest as you've a mind to, but, if I was you, I'd dreen.'

So they drained it long and crossways in the lavish Roman style –
Still we find among the river-drift their flakes of ancient tile,
And in drouthy middle August, when the bones of meadows show,
We can trace the lines they followed sixteen hundred years ago.

Then Julius Fabricius died as even Prefects do,
And after certain centuries, Imperial Rome died too.
Then did robbers enter Britain from across the Northern main
And our Lower River-field was won by Ogier the Dane.

Well could Ogier work his war-boat – well could Ogier wield his brand –
Much he knew of foaming waters – not so much of farming land.
So he called to him a Hobden of the old unaltered blood,
Saying: 'What about that River-piece; she doesn't look no good?'

And that aged Hobden answered: ' 'Tain't for *me* to interfere,
But I've known that bit o' meadow now for five and fifty year.
Have it *jest* as you've a mind to, but I've proved it time on time,
If you want to change her nature you have *got* to give her lime!'

Ogier sent his wains to Lewes, twenty hours' solemn walk,
And drew back great abundance of the cool, grey, healing chalk.
And old Hobden spread it broadcast, never heeding what was in't. –
Which is why in cleaning ditches, now and then we find a flint.

Ogier died. His sons grew English – Anglo-Saxon was their name –
Till out of blossomed Normandy another pirate came;
For Duke William conquered England and divided with his men,
And our Lower River-field he gave to William of Warenne.

But the Brook (you know her habit) rose one rainy autumn night
And tore down sodden flitches of the bank to left and right.
So, said William to his Bailiff as they rode their dripping rounds:
'Hob, what about that River-bit – the Brook's got up no bounds?'

And that aged Hobden answered: ' 'Tain't my business to advise,
But ye might ha' known 'twould happen from the way the valley lies.
Where ye can't hold back the water you must try and save the sile.
Hev it jest as you've a *mind* to, but, if I was you, I'd spile!'

They spiled along the water-course with trunks of willow-trees,
And planks of elms behind 'em and immortal oaken knees.
And when the spates of Autumn whirl the gravel-beds away
You can see their faithful fragments, iron-hard in iron clay.

.   .   .   .

Georgii Quinti Anno Sexto, I, who own the River-field,
Am fortified with title-deeds, attested, signed and sealed,
Guaranteeing me, my assigns, my executors and heirs
All sorts of powers and profits which – are neither mine nor theirs.

I have rights of chase and warren, as my dignity requires.
I can fish – but Hobden tickles. I can shoot – but Hobden wires.
I repair, but he reopens, certain gaps which, men allege,
Have been used by every Hobden since a Hobden swapped a hedge.

Shall I dog his morning progress o'er the track-betraying dew?
Demand his dinner-basket into which my pheasant flew?
Confiscate his evening faggot under which my conies ran,
And summons him to judgment? I would sooner summons Pan.

His dead are in the churchyard – thirty generations laid.
Their names were old in history when Domesday Book was made;
And the passion and the piety and prowess of his line
Have seeded, rooted, fruited in some land the Law calls mine.

Not for any beast that burrows, not for any bird that flies,
Would I lose his large sound counsel, miss his keen amending eyes.
He is bailiff, woodman, wheelwright, field-surveyor, engineer,
And if flagrantly a poacher – 'tain't for me to interfere.

'Hob, what about that River-bit?' I turn to him again,
With Fabricius and Ogier and William of Warenne.
'Hev it jest as you've a mind to, *but*' – and here he takes command.
For whoever pays the taxes old Mus' Hobden owns the land.

Illustrations from the Luttrell Psalter

nus :꞉ ꞇ rex magnus super omnes
deos.

ꞇ herit dommo ꞇ laur gentium ar
ferte dommo gloriam ꞇ honorem :

Quoniam tu dominus attuïmus
super omnem terram : nimis exalta
tus es super omnes deos.

INDEX OF FIRST LINES

[118]

ACKNOWLEDGEMENTS

British Printing Corporation, back cover (middle); British Museum, front cover (middle),
back cover (bottom); Guildhall Museum, 29; Michael Holford, front cover (top); Imperial
War Museum, front cover (bottom); Mansell Collection, 2, 13, 22, 117 (centre); New York
Public Library, 61; Radio Times Hulton Picture Library, 3, 54–5, 72–3, 96, 109; Royal
Commission on Historical Monuments, 11; Royal Geographical Society, 46; Universitets
Oldsaksamling, Oslo, 20; Victoria and Albert Museum, 23, 30, 33, 35, 41, 43, 66, 74, 99;
Roger Viollet, 69; Warburg Institute, 17; Zefa, back cover (top).

The illustrations on the front cover, reading from the top, show: The Franks casket,
whalebone; a detail from the Bradford table carpet; John Singer Sergeant's painting
Gassed. The back cover illustrations show: Trajan's Column; a Carolingian manuscript
illustration; another detail from the Bradford table carpet.